CLARKSTON INDEPENDENCE DISTRICT LIBRARY
W9-APZ-395
WITHDRAWN

"Karen González weaves together a brilliant book that illuminates how central the stories of immigrants are to the story of God. This is true not just in the Scriptures but also today, as Karen beautifully illustrates when she describes how God drew her close. Immigration is often talked about as a policy or political issue, and this book is a sorely needed reminder that immigration is a personal issue—one that can connect us all to the heart and mission of God."

JENNY YANG, vice president of advocacy and policy at World Relief and coauthor of *Welcoming the Stranger*

"With this stunning debut, Karen González makes her mark as one of the most talented storytellers of faith in a generation. The skill with which she weaves together personal narrative, biblical text, intimate detail, and sociopolitical analysis is as impressive as it is seamless. Every single page of this beautiful, timely book pulses with prophetic truth. It left me changed in all the best ways."

RACHEL HELD EVANS, author of *Inspired* and *Searching for Sunday*

"We are changed by whom we read the Bible with. The God Who Sees *is an invitation to read the Scriptures with the fresh eyes of Karen González, a theologian with a story that is relevant, heartbreaking, and always surprising. González deeply believes in* the God who sees, *and she invites her readers to discover the God who is obsessed with the immigrant. In a time of fear,* The God Who Sees *is a powerful testimony to what makes the good news actually good."*

D. L. MAYFIELD, author of *Assimilate or Go Home*

CLARKSTON INDEPENDENCE
DISTRICT LIBRARY
6495 CLARKSTON ROAD
CLARKSTON, MI 48346-1501

"The God Who Sees *artfully weaves theological application and immigration policy and practice, inviting the reader to engage more deeply in important justice issues of today. At a time in which numerous voices are being pushed into the immigration narrative, Karen González's perspectives as a theologian and Latina immigrant, straddling Guatemalan and American cultures, are both insightful and impactful. Thank you, Karen, for sharing your heart, your mind, and your voice in this book. It is a gift."*

MICHELLE FERRIGNO WARREN, activist and author of *The Power of Proximity*

"The topic of immigration can be both confusing and contentious. Karen González helps us find our way toward a deeper understanding with The God Who Sees, *a story that is deeply personal, solidly biblical, and appropriately challenging. You will find Karen González an able guide to bring clarity and encourage compassion."*

SCOTT ARBEITER, president of World Relief

"Weaving insightful reflections on the stories of immigrants in the Bible, compelling explanations of the realities facing immigrants today, and her own testimony of faith and migration, Karen González invites readers into a distinctly Christian approach to the complex topic of immigration. In the process, she invites us into a deeper relationship with the God who made and loves them. The God Who Sees *is an important and enlightening book for our times."*

MATTHEW SOERENS, coauthor of *Welcoming the Stranger* and *Seeking Refuge*

"In this engaging book, Karen González skillfully weaves her narrative with the biblical narratives and insightful comments on current immigration realities. This slim volume is a helpful introduction for those who want to love their immigrant neighbors. I appreciated the action and reflection questions that end the book and offer helpful next steps."

JUDE TIERSMA WATSON, associate professor at Fuller Theological Seminary

"What does it mean to surrender our lives to the God of the immigrant and stranger? That question feels more pressing than ever in our modern times. The God Who Sees *takes us on a journey that brings us to the heart of God and shapes a new way of seeing the world. Trust the leadership of Karen González, an important spiritual guide for these critical conversations."*

DANIEL HILL, pastor and author of *White Awake*

"The God Who Sees *is the book I have been waiting for: a Christian book on immigration, written from the perspective of a Latina theologian and ministry practitioner, that centers the voices and experiences of our Latino community. It is like refreshing water to my soul. Karen González stands at the vanguard of a rising generation of Latina/o Christian authors whose voices are critical for the healing of the church in America."*

ROBERT CHAO ROMERO, professor of Chicana/o studies at UCLA

"The God Who Sees *offers the powerful combination of an immigrant experience expressed through the lens of Scripture. Nothing can be more compelling for those who claim the Christian faith. As a fellow Guatemalan American, I resonate with this book that brings to mind my own memories and their emotive power. Karen González's voice is gentle, yet forceful, and needs to be heard—along with those of millions of others!"*

M. DANIEL CARROLL R., professor of Old Testament at Wheaton College and author of *Christians at the Border*

"The God Who Sees *is a beautiful, timely, and significant book. Karen González's unique interweaving of personal story and biblical story, as well as her expertise in immigration services, provides substantial information for believers seeking to understand migration at this historic moment. The book takes complex concepts and makes them easily accessible. A must-read for Christian believers seeking God's will for churches grappling with immigration issues."*

ALEXIA SALVATIERRA, author of *Faith-Rooted Organizing*

"In The God Who Sees, *we who are identified as immigrants, migrants, refugees, and asylum seekers find that God is at work in our stories and in the narratives of foreigners and strangers in the Bible. With intimacy and detail, author Karen González reminds us of the importance of migration stories and how God is present in our uprooting, our journeys, our language and assimilation challenges, and our unceasing longing for home. She has written a timely memoir of us, for us, and for our sons and daughters."*

SAULO PADILLA, coordinator of the Immigration Education National Program at Mennonite Central Committee U.S.

"In the heated debate over immigration, both sides often reduce immigrants to an abstraction. Karen González points out that the story of the immigrant is an integral part of our redemption history. Her own journey as an immigrant adds rich insight to our collective faith story as well as a deeper understanding of those millions who still leave their homes in search of new lives. The God Who Sees *will convict the reader that compassion for the immigrant is not an option but a requirement for all who profess to follow Jesus."*

DEREK W. ENGDAHL, author of *The Great Chasm*

THE GOD WHO SEES

THE GOD WHO SEES

Immigrants, the Bible,
and the Journey to Belong

KAREN GONZÁLEZ

Harrisonburg, Virginia

Herald Press
PO Box 866, Harrisonburg, Virginia 22803
www.HeraldPress.com

Library of Congress Cataloging-in-Publication Data
Names: González, Karen (Karen J.), author.
Title: The God who sees : immigrants, the Bible, and the journey to belong / Karen González.
Description: Harrisonburg, Virginia : Herald Press, [2019] | Includes bibliographical references.
Identifiers: LCCN 2018056925| ISBN 9781513804132 (hardcover : alk. paper) | ISBN 9781513804125 (pbk. : alk. paper) | ISBN 9781513804149 (ebk.)
Subjects: LCSH: Emigration and immigration in the Bible. | Emigration and immigration--Religious aspects--Christianity. | González, Karen (Karen J.) | Immigrants--United States--Biography. | Hispanic American women--Biography. | Christian women--United States--Biography.
Classification: LCC BS680.E38 G66 2019 | DDC 277.3/083092 [B] --dc23 LC record available at https://lccn.loc.gov/2018056925

THE GOD WHO SEES
© 2019 by Herald Press, Harrisonburg, Virginia 22803. 800-245-7894. All rights reserved.
Library of Congress Control Number: 2018056925
International Standard Book Number: 978-1-5138-0412-5 (paperback); 978-1-5138-0413-2 (hardcover); 978-1-5138-0414-9 (ebook)
Printed in United States of America
Cover and interior design by Reuben Graham

All rights reserved. This publication may not be reproduced, stored in a retrieval system, or transmitted in whole or in part, in any form, by any means, electronic, mechanical, photocopying, recording or otherwise without prior permission of the copyright owners.

Unless otherwise noted, Scripture quotations in this publication are from the Common English Bible. © 2011 by the Common English Bible. All rights reserved. Used by permission.

Scripture quotations in Spanish identified (RVR 1960) are taken from KJV™ © 1960 Latin American Bible Society, 1960. Rights renewed 1988 United Bible Societies.

23 22 21 20 19 10 9 8 7 6 5 4 3 2 1

3 4633 00337 9284

To my mother and father, Myra Teresa Tally de González and Jorge Luis González Santo, whose deep commitment to the well-being of their children led them to leave their native Guatemala. They have given me an inspiring example of sacrificial love.

Contents

Foreword *13*
Preface *17*

1 Naomi and Ruth: A Blessed Alliance. 21
2 Baptism. 37
3 Abraham: The Immigrant Father of Our Faith. 49
4 Communion 61
5 Hagar: The "Foreign Thing" and the God Who Sees Her 73
6 Confirmation 85
7 Joseph: The Foreigner Who Blessed Egypt 97
8 Anointing the Sick 111
9 The Syrophoenician Woman: The Foreigner with Sass. 123
10 Reconciliation 139
11 The Holy Family: Our Refugee Savior and a Love with No Limits 151

Ideas for Action and Reflection *165*
Discussion Questions. *173*
Acknowledgments *187*
Notes *191*
The Author. *199*

Foreword

I waited to take an ethics course until my last year of seminary. As a pastor and activist, I craved learning that resulted in visible impact much more than abstract theory. So when I saw on my ethics syllabus that we were going to address social ethics such as immigration, I was thrilled.

Initially. Imagine my disappointment when I learned that migration and immigration would be the topic not of lectures but rather of an assigned paper so that we could explore it on an individual basis. Wait. No discussions, no arguments, no influencing one another in class? How could a topic of such incredible importance not be given at least *one* class when the other topics—about the beginning of life, and sexuality, and the end of life—were given three?

In the end, immigration wasn't even assigned as a mandatory topic for our papers. Apparently immigration was "not an issue" in all contexts of ministry. Future pastors were given permission to opt out of exploring ethical issues of loving their neighbors. Policies that affect so many disenfranchised communities in the United States were, apparently, not considered important issues for the church.

The story of Scripture is the story of displaced people. *The God Who Sees* would have convinced my professor and other students that at the center of biblical ethics is love for the Other. This fantastic study of Scripture, which also offers information on immigration policy, invites us to understand that caring for our neighbor requires acts of compassion and mercy as well as the pursuit of just policies. As Justo González says in his commentary on the book of Luke, "Justice requires a reversal of conditions for the excluded and oppressed." We must be biblically motivated, sociologically informed, and practically invited to love and welcome the stranger. Showing hospitality is not only for the benefit of the "stranger" but for the mutuality and strengthening of the church.

My classmates had sat in Old Testament Hebrew and New Testament Greek with me. We had studied the same Scriptures, and they were future pastors and church leaders. Yet somehow they had missed that Abraham, Isaac, Jacob, Moses, Ruth, David, Mary, Joseph, and Jesus were all economic and political refugees and asylum seekers. My friends were not mean, but because they were not in proximity to the kinds of stories we were reading in the Bible, they saw immigrants in Scripture as disembodied characters who represented spiritual realities rather than as real foreigners and aliens with whom God had been traveling all along. Immigrant and refugee children detained, incarcerated, and trafficked were thus seen as optional "political" issues to speak to, but not part of their daily realities as future pastors. Speaking truth to power on immigration policy was seen as elective, not a responsibility.

I share this story not to discredit my friends but as an illustration of the problem that the church faces in our generation. We operate in a disembodied spirituality that understands reading Scripture as merely a way to know God's character rather than as a way of seeing God's particular acts of mercy, compassion, and justice. God acted on behalf of displaced people. God centers the foreigner and alien not only in God's words (see Deuteronomy 10) but also in the story of Scripture itself. In the Old Testament, we see this through the acts of God and the words of the prophets. In the New Testament, we see this in the life and words of Jesus, who says that love of neighbor is a sign of our realized love for God.

Karen González offers us a compelling biblical case for the centrality of God's work on behalf of the foreigner. She reminds us, through her own modern immigrant story, that we need a reorientation of the entire biblical narrative. From Abraham in Genesis through our refugee King in the story of the Holy Family, Scripture helps us see the God who sees more accurately than we ever can.

God's people are knocking on our doors, asking us to let them help us be the church God always intended us to be. González's expertise and wisdom alert us to the reality that if we as twenty-first-century Western Christians really want to know God, we must pay attention to immigrants—not for their conversion, but for ours.

—**Sandra Maria Van Opstal**, pastor, activist, and author of *The Next Worship*

Preface

I was inspired to write this book because so few books about immigrants are written by immigrants themselves. I kept wondering aloud to my family and friends why more of us were not telling our own stories in the pages of books. I kept insisting that just as Alexander Hamilton's perspective adds richness and depth to the story of the United States, as fans of Lin-Manuel Miranda's *Hamilton* know so well, so would immigrant stories, told by immigrants, provide a personal and intimate perspective on the subject. After months of hearing me complain, a friend gently suggested, "Why don't *you* write that book?"

So it was that I began to pray and seek God about writing a book—a thought that had never seriously entered my mind. Over that time, I felt more and more spurred by the Holy Spirit to begin this project: to tell the story in a way it had not been told before, weaving personal narrative, information on immigration policy and trends, and the retelling of immigrant stories found in the Bible.

In a way, I felt that God had been preparing me to tell this story for my whole life. I majored in literature at my university and spent my young adulthood immersed in beautiful storytelling. I went to seminary, where I learned to locate the books of the Bible in their historical context and to interpret the Bible with various lenses. And I work for a nonprofit organization, World Relief, which works in immigrant legal services and refugee resettlement. It seemed to me that God was using my unique background to provide an important and needed perspective.

Because I am both a Christian and an immigrant, I wanted to write about the Bible and what it says about immigration. It was important for me to communicate that the story of immigrants is told in the Bible. God wasn't silent on the subject of immigration; in fact, God gave strict instructions on how immigrants should be treated, providing specific protections for us. And Jesus himself was a refugee for a time, a baby whose parents fled their homeland for safety.

In the pages of this book, you'll find an immigration story and biblical reflections. Every other chapter is my own immigration story told through five of the sacraments in the Roman Catholic Church: baptism, communion, confirmation, anointing the sick, and reconciliation. I realize that likely seems odd to many readers, since I'm no longer a Catholic but a Protestant Christian. I chose the sacraments because they are visible signs of an inward grace, and because the Catholic sacraments shaped my early imagination of faith. I also learned through the writing of this book how much my immigrant experience informs my understanding of God.

Because this book is part memoir, I have to confess that my memory is not always trustworthy, but I have done my best to share what is true and accurate. Some of the names of people outside my family, as well as details about their lives, have been changed for privacy, and a few represent composite stories that we hear frequently at World Relief's immigration clinic.

It's also important to note that while I learned much about immigration processes and petitions while working at an immigration legal clinic at World Relief, this book should not be used or relied on as a legal guide for your own immigration process. If you're in the United States, the Department of Justice offers a list of pro bono and low-cost immigration legal service providers who are accredited and reputable. I encourage anyone to find an attorney or accredited representative to serve their needs. And if you're in the Baltimore area, I know a few places I can highly recommend.

On a final note, while I was writing this book, I would often run into people who, in an effort to affirm me and this project, would tell me that this was an important book to write *right now*—in our current political climate, which is so unwelcoming to immigrants. Many would encourage me to hurry up and get it on the market because it's critical *at this political moment*. I was grateful for the affirmation, but I want to push back on one aspect of their encouragement. That is, the story of belonging is always an important story. Immigrant stories *always* matter, because immigrants are image-bearers of God. God alone endows us with value and dignity, and centers our stories. As such, they are always important stories to tell. Always.

Thank you so much for reading this book! It is truly a labor of love for my immigrant community in North America, which has suffered so much in our political climate with both its violent rhetoric and its unwelcoming policies. It is an honor to share this story with you.

1

Naomi and Ruth

A Blessed Alliance

Your people will be my people, and your God will be my God.
—RUTH 1:16

I first heard of the book of Ruth when I was in college. I was at a friend's house for a small group meeting for my college fellowship. As we were waiting for everyone else to arrive, I happened to see an intricately embroidered picture hanging on the wall. In the foreground stood a bride and groom in all their wedding finery. Behind them was a little country church with colorful stained glass windows. Embroidered below the church were these words: "Where you go I will go, and where you stay I will stay. Your people will be my people and your God my God. Ruth 1:16."

My friend saw me looking at the picture. "Somebody gave that to my sister for her wedding," he explained.

"I didn't know there was a book in the Bible named after a woman!" I blurted out. Generally, I like to be in the know, and I didn't like to let on that I knew very little about the Bible. It was embarrassing. But this passage had caught me by surprise.

"Yeah, there are a couple," my friend said. "This one is in the Old Testament. It foreshadows Jesus through a man named Boaz, who is the 'kinsman redeemer'—a kind of stand-in for Jesus. But it's also about love and loyalty. So this passage is a popular reading at weddings."

The conversation shifted then, and I was left alone with my thoughts.

At that time I had very little experience reading the Bible, and much less in understanding anything I read. But this passage didn't seem to require much explanation, and it did indeed seem a beautiful sentiment for a wedding, speaking not just of love and loyalty but also of steadfastness and faithfulness.

Since then I've discovered that most children's Sunday school books portray the story of Ruth almost like a Disney princess tale: Ruth is the poor maiden, Naomi is the fairy godmother always looking out for her best interest, and Boaz is the knight in shining armor who saves the day. That version is a quaint little Bible story in which all the main characters—Ruth, Naomi, and Boaz—do everything right. That's what my friend described when I saw the embroidered picture on his family's wall. He believed this was a story about a heroic man who sweeps in on a white horse to save the damsels in distress.

But when I went home and read the short four chapters of the book of Ruth, I found that those words, spoken by Ruth to her mother-in-law, Naomi, have nothing to do with marriage or even a romantic relationship. In fact, these words were not ones spoken during the best of times, like a wedding or the birth of a child.

No. These words were spoken by one widow to another during the worst of times, after a series of devastating losses: infertility, death, widowhood, abject poverty, and forced migration. It wasn't what I had thought at all.

It wasn't until many years later that I fell in love with this Old Testament book. Only years after that small group meeting did I realize how deeply I, as a woman and an immigrant, resonated with the story. The book of Ruth is one of the few places in the Bible where immigrants are treated just as God's law commands: "When immigrants live in your land with you, you must not cheat them. Any immigrant who lives with you must be treated as if they were one of your citizens. You must love them as yourself, because you were immigrants in the land of Egypt; I am the Lord your God" (Leviticus 19:33-34).

As an immigrant, I am loved and seen by the holy God of the universe. Our Bible, inspired by God, includes an entire book that deals directly with the just treatment and acceptance of the foreigner. In the many churches I had attended since my childhood, I had never heard that the Scriptures have something to say about the way that immigrants—people like my family and me—should be treated. I had never heard that the Bible commands that we be regarded as native citizens, treated fairly, and even loved like family.

Naomi and Elimelech, economic immigrants

In the biblical text, we learn that the story of Ruth begins in Bethlehem, a name that means "house of bread." But there's no more bread in the house. There's a famine in the land, and it's severe enough and lasts long enough that people begin to migrate in search of food.

A man named Elimelech and his wife, Naomi, immigrate to Moab, a neighboring country, with their two sons, Mahlon and Chilion. There, these economic immigrants find the food they need and decide to stay and build a life for themselves. For many years, the immigrant life is good: food is plentiful, and their young sons grow into manhood and marry local Moabite women, Orpah and Ruth.

But quite suddenly their fortunes change. Elimelech dies, and as if that were not bad enough, the young sons soon die too, without leaving any heirs. Although Naomi's sons were married for more than ten years, neither of their Moabite wives were able to have children, and now both women are widows along with their mother-in-law. This all happens in the first five verses of chapter 1! As a woman who had seen so many of the women in my family fight for survival when tragedy befell them, I was intrigued. Clearly, this was going to be a story not about dead men but about the survival of women.

But Ruth and Naomi's survival is doubtful. Though God has specifically outlined care for vulnerable people in the law—people like widows, orphans, immigrants, and the poor—those laws were given to God's people, Israel, and even God's people don't always follow them. Life often does not work out well for people like Naomi and her daughters-in-law. It's altogether possible that Moab provides no protection for widows and other vulnerable people. So these women are, indeed, in a precarious situation. The ancient world is an agrarian society, in which widows, orphans, immigrants, and the poor have no economic or social power and live at the subsistence level. If a tragedy like a famine, a drought, or a foreign invasion strikes, they are the first to suffer and perish.[1] It's not unlike today, when the elderly, the homeless, single parents, and refugees are particularly vulnerable to poverty, abuse, or early death.

But amid all the tragedy, good news soon reaches Naomi: there's food again in Bethlehem! She can return home and find the sustenance that she needs among her own people. She decides to return and take her daughters-in-law with her. But just as suddenly, she changes her mind and decides the two young women should stay behind after all. Maybe since her daughters-in-law aren't pregnant with sons, they're of no use to Naomi—just more mouths to feed. Maybe she remembers the challenges and trials of being an immigrant and doesn't want to put her beloved daughters-in-law through the same thing. Just as they do today, immigrants in the ancient world often experienced xenophobia, suspicion, and verbal and physical abuse. Or maybe Naomi remembers that, no matter how much she loves her daughters-in-law, the Israelites despise their Moabite neighbors.

For there is lots of strife between Moab and Judah. Moabites are part of Abraham's extended family, descended from the incestuous union of Lot and his daughters in Genesis. In fact, Israel's disdain for their Moabite cousins can be seen in Deuteronomy 23:3, in which Moabites were excluded from the assembly of the Lord for ten generations and beyond. And they're not just excluded from the assembly; Nehemiah 13 states emphatically that a child of Israel is forbidden to marry a Moabite. So Naomi would have rightly feared how her daughters-in-law would be received in Judah. History told her not to expect a warm welcome for them.

Whatever Naomi's reasons, she manages to convince one of her daughters-in-law, Orpah, to stay. Orpah is sensible and decides to remain with her own people, perhaps realizing that her best chance at remarriage is within her own culture. But Ruth is undeterred. Some might even say that she is irrationally faithful. Theologian Megan McKenna notes, "Ruth sides with Naomi and gives her life to Naomi in love and friendship, leaving everything to make her mother-in-law's life easier. She pledges her life even unto death to her."[2] Theirs will be a story of surviving or perishing, but Ruth will remain with Naomi come what may. She speaks her famous words of love and loyalty and renews her commitment never to abandon Naomi (see Ruth 1:16-17).

Sometimes I've wondered if Naomi, seeing Ruth's love and commitment to her, feels like many of the elderly Americans my mother took care of as a home healthcare worker in the United States. While their relatives couldn't care for them, my mother did so until their deaths. She offered them companionship and care, listening to their stories. Naomi faces an uncertain future, but she is not alone. She is with a woman, Ruth, who loves and cares for her deeply.

I can only imagine how painful and humiliating the trot into Bethlehem must have been for Naomi. She hadn't left under great circumstances, of course; there had been a famine, and all the uncertainties that accompany it. But at least she'd had a husband and young sons by her side back then, a woman's only assurance of security. Now she is coming back ten years older, and she literally has nothing except an empty belly. Beside her trudges another grieving widow—a barren woman, a foreigner, another person she'd have to take care of in her hometown.

This is not the triumphant homecoming she had dreamed of through all those years in Moab, the type of homecoming immigrants still long for today. The two times my entire family returned to Guatemala after we migrated to the United States were filled with joyful celebration at our arrival. Friends and family hired marimba bands and hosted parties for us, and my parents brought gifts for everyone. These are the kind of homecomings that immigrants dream of, when they return happier and better off. But Naomi's return is enveloped in grief and loss.

Ruth, the immigrant

But the timing of their arrival couldn't be better, given their circumstances. It's the beginning of the barley harvest. As an Israelite, Naomi likely knows this is an opportune time to return because of God's command in the law to provide for vulnerable people:

> Whenever you are reaping the harvest of your field and you leave some grain in the field, don't go back and get it. *Let it go to the immigrants, the orphans, and the widows* so that the Lord your God blesses you in all that you do. Similarly,

> when you beat the olives off your olive trees, don't go back over them twice. Let the leftovers go to the *immigrants, the orphans, and the widows*. Again, when you pick the grapes of your vineyard, don't pick them over twice. Let the leftovers go to *the immigrants, the orphans, and the widows*. (Deuteronomy 24:19-21, italics mine)

Indeed, in the story of Ruth we find this command carried out. Naomi and Ruth's story reveals a vision of a whole community that cares for immigrants and others in vulnerable situations.

The immigrant, Ruth, is welcomed onto the field of Boaz, a relative of Naomi's, although Ruth has no knowledge of this fact at the time. There she gleans what the regular harvesters left behind, just as the Scriptures said, and brings it home to her mother-in-law. Boaz knows that even this immigrant from a despised community is entitled to work for her livelihood. He provides her with a decent job and a decent living. And the work Ruth performs is not undignified or demeaning; it is hard work, just as all agricultural work is, but it is exactly the kind of work that most people did in the world of ancient Judah. Ruth isn't doing the work that nobody else is willing to do. Many immigrants today spend long hours in fields, slaughterhouses, and warehouses, doing the backbreaking work few others are willing to do. But Ruth is welcomed onto Boaz's field to do the work any citizen in need would have done.

And Ruth is entitled not just to a job but also to respect. Boaz reminds his workers that there is to be no harassment and no sexual or physical assault (see Ruth 2:9, 15). Being a poor immigrant doesn't mean that she should endure humiliation and mistreatment. Today, many immigrant women have no such protection. Most immigrant women working in agriculture have been sexually assaulted or know a woman who has been. Many view it as an unavoidable condition of this kind of work.[3] But Boaz makes sure that Ruth is safe and is treated as respectfully as any one of his workers.

He also invites Ruth to his table, where she breaks bread with him and his workers. She drinks from the water containers filled by the harvesters, and she is satisfied and has leftovers for Naomi and herself. She is allowed the same rights and privileges as a native Judean. Boaz practices true hospitality—*philoxenia*, as it's called in the New Testament. *Philoxenia* is a love of strangers and foreigners.

And both Ruth and Boaz are entitled to Sabbath: time off for rest, reflection, celebration, and worship. Boaz surely knows that in Exodus a strict command was given for Sabbath:

> Keep the Sabbath day and treat it as holy, exactly as the Lord your God commanded: six days you may work and do all your tasks, but the seventh day is a Sabbath to the Lord your God. Don't do any work on it—not you, your sons or daughters, your male or female servants, your oxen or donkeys or any of your animals, *or the immigrant who is living among you*—so that your male and female servants can rest just like you. (Deuteronomy 5:12-14, italics mine)

God is very concerned with providing rest for those who can't secure it for themselves and wants the people to remember that the Sabbath was created for everyone, not just the Israelites. All creatures, including enslaved people, immigrants, and even animals, are invited into a weekly day of rest. So it is that Ruth rests one day a week, along with the people of Judah.

The story of Boaz?

Readers of this passage often focus on Boaz's kindness and generosity. It's true that Boaz shows both those qualities—his generosity of spirit is unparalleled. But what is usually overlooked is the fact that, as a follower of the God of Israel, Boaz is actually *not* free to act in any other way. Boaz simply does what God's law commands. It is *God's law* that guarantees Ruth a place in gleaning his crops: "He enacts justice for orphans and widows, and he loves immigrants, giving them food and clothing. That means you must also love immigrants because you were immigrants in Egypt" (Deuteronomy 10:18-19).

All the people in the margins of society, not just Ruth, have the right to simply walk onto a field and begin to work for their livelihood. And Boaz has an obligation not to order his regular workers to harvest everything for his own economic gain. They cannot harvest what grows in the corners of the field, nor what they missed on the first time around. Compassion for those who are poor and marginalized is considered more important than efficiency or profit. And it's clear that Boaz shows compassion to all in need, because he extends it to Ruth even before he knows she is Naomi's daughter-in-law.

While the story of Ruth is often retold as a Disney fairy tale, such a reading of this story robs Naomi and Ruth of agency. It removes the choices and actions that empower them to labor with God for their flourishing. Yes, it's true that Ruth and Naomi are poor and vulnerable. But they are not helpless. They conspire for their survival, writes McKenna, as they share "love, history, and hope together."[4]

A blessed alliance

If you look closely at the dynamics that lie behind the story, you'll see another dimension—something theologian Carolyn Custis James has called "the blessed alliance." A blessed alliance occurs when women and men work together for the flourishing of the world. According to Genesis, writes James, "male/female relationships are a kingdom strategy—designed to be an unstoppable force for good in the world."[5]

Everyone in the story of Ruth has something to offer:

Ruth may be a poor, immigrant widow, but she is a hard worker. The text tells us she gleans and threshes until evening, collecting about twenty quarts of threshed barley. She's also socially savvy and compassionate. Ruth boldly but appropriately makes herself known to Boaz—in fact, most biblical scholars say she makes the first move in their eventual relationship! She also takes good care of her mother-in-law. And her love and loyalty to Naomi earn her Boaz's favor.

Naomi may be poor and too old to work, but she is a cultural insider. Because she's an Israelite, she knows how to navigate the laws of the land—the law that provides for the poor and the immigrant, and the law that says her closest relative must come to her aid. As a woman and a widow, she's powerless to enforce these laws, but she helps Ruth to understand the system and to position herself in such a way as to benefit from it. She could have chosen to have Ruth work and provide for her, but instead she shows Ruth how to make her way in the society of Judah. She teaches Ruth about the culture of this new land she inhabits.

And then there's Boaz. As a man and a landowner, Boaz is the most powerful of the three. Providentially, he understands the biblical use of power for the common good. Rather than reveling in his own privilege, exploiting his workers, or caring only for his own people, he chooses justice and compassion. Offering Ruth an honest means to earn a living while providing a safe work environment for her, he cares for the immigrant widow. And he does so long before there's any benefit for him—long before there's any promise of marriage between them.

My friend was partly correct when he stated that the story of Ruth is about a kinsman redeemer: a type of Jesus figure who steps up to his responsibility as Naomi's relative through her husband, Elimelech. But it's also the story of a family of immigrants who find refuge in Moab. Mostly, however, it's the story of an immigrant woman: a woman who arrives in Judah and is welcomed and accepted as one of Judah's own. It's the story of an immigrant woman who leaves her own country, language, and culture out of love for her elderly mother-in-law. Theologians have even noted that it is an outsider who teaches the people of Judah what true love and loyalty can look like.[6]

Ruth at the border

I wish that all immigrant stories ended like Ruth's. But having worked at World Relief, an organization that resettles refugees and provides immigrants with legal services, I know better. "If Ruth came to America today, what would happen to her?" asks Rabbi Arthur Waskow. "Would she be admitted at the border?"[7]

One needs only a limited knowledge of U.S. and Canadian immigration laws to know that she wouldn't. According to the U.S. Citizenship and Immigration Services, Ruth, despite her poverty, could not be classified as a refugee or asylee. Those statuses are reserved strictly for those who have been persecuted or fear they will be persecuted on account of race, religion, nationality, political opinion, or membership in a particular social group.[8] Fleeing because of famine or widowhood doesn't fall under any of those categories.

Ruth also wouldn't qualify for the diversity visa lottery, which is an immigrant visa open to those in countries underrepresented among U.S. immigrant groups. Only those with a high school diploma qualify for that opportunity. We don't know much about Ruth's education, but chances are good that, as a woman, she has little or no education.

Many immigrants migrate legally to the United States because they're sponsored by relatives who are U.S. citizens. It's called family-based migration, and it's an essential part of the United States' current immigration system. But Ruth also wouldn't qualify for sponsorship through Naomi, her mother-in-law, because citizens may only sponsor their spouse, parents, children, or siblings.[9] Having lost her citizen husband and having a mother-in-law with no income would make sponsorship impossible. Even if Naomi found a loophole in the law, she could never present the government with proof that Ruth would never become a public charge, because Naomi doesn't work. Furthermore, the wait for a sponsorship visa for someone who is not a spouse, a child under the age of twenty-one, or a parent is currently anywhere from twelve to twenty-three years.

Ruth's only hope might be a temporary work visa, but there are very few of those offered each year, in comparison to the number of immigrants who apply for them. Most often these are awarded to doctors, software engineers, and other professionals whose skills might be challenging to find in the United States. Though there might be a few visas available for unskilled agricultural workers, these visas have many restrictions. And as their name implies, they are temporary.

I shudder to think of the blessing Judah would have missed had it had the kind of border control and immigration process that the United States has. As a family-based economic immigrant, Ruth would have no recourse. Today she would return to Moab alone. Today she would be turned away at the border, while the elderly Naomi would go on, hoping for the mercy of a relative to care for her.

The immigration system in the United States stands in sharp contrast to what we see in the little book of Ruth. There we see a picture of the immigrant and the citizen working together, side by side, for the flourishing of their communities. The concern isn't just for their own security or economic interest. Nobody looks out just for their own country or ethnic group. Nobody considers themselves superior and subjugates the powerless.

In the story of Ruth, human beings become their best selves, and as a result, everyone thrives, not just survives. The book of Ruth is a beautiful narrative with a very happy ending: as listed in the lineage of Jesus in Matthew 1, Obed, the son of the immigrant Ruth and the citizen Boaz, eventually becomes the grandfather of King David.

2

Baptism

All of you who were baptized into Christ have clothed yourselves with Christ.
—**GALATIANS 3:27**

The first voices I ever heard were in Spanish. I don't remember them, of course, but I know they were the voices of my mother, my father, and my tía Mocle, who took care of me in Guatemala, where I was born and where I lived until I was nine years old. Somewhere around the time I was six months old, I also heard the voice of a Catholic priest at my baptism. I don't remember his voice.

I would love to say that my parents believed the words the priest spoke over me, or that my baptism as an infant signified a momentous occasion in my life of faith. I would love to say that my parents were initiating me into the church of Jesus

Christ and that they were conferring on me a faith they hoped I would make my own someday. But that was not the case.

My parents were nominal Christians, although maybe not even that. My father came from a Catholic family. He was a socialist who not only did not believe in God but believed the church was a crutch for weak-minded people, one that kept the poor oppressed by sanctifying their suffering. When I was a baby, my father placed a picture of Che Guevara, the socialist revolutionary, on the wall above my crib, much to my tía Mocle's disapproval. Mostly, my father believed in making the world a better place; you could say his faith was in humankind.

In contrast, my mother's family was Protestant: evangelical Afro-Latinxs from Guatemala's Caribbean coast. My abuelita Amada was a faithful Christian but also a bit of a zealous and legalist one—so much so that she had driven most of her own children away from any kind of faith pursuit. On more than one occasion I heard my mother proclaim that it was fine to believe in God, but there was no need to get fanatical about it. But knowing how much my abuelita disapproved of Catholicism, my mother did not even tell her about my Catholic baptism. My parents held beliefs, but what they believed in were traditions and celebrations. It was with those experiences in their backgrounds that they had me baptized into the Roman Catholic Church.

While I have no recollection of my own baptism, I do remember being present at my brother's and sister's baptisms, which happened on the same day. It was a solemn and serious event at a Catholic church in Guatemala City. My cousin held my little sister over the baptismal font while the priest poured water over her head and said, "En el nombre del Padre, del Hijo, y del Espíritu Santo" (In the name of the Father, the Son, and the Holy Spirit). Michelle was one year old, and she did not like water on her face, so she shook her little head and wiped it all away with her hands. Then my brother was held over the baptismal font and the actions and words were repeated. None of us understood the significance of baptism then. I was seven, and the ceremony was long and involved. Aside from the sprinkling, I mostly remember my new dress and shiny patent leather shoes.

What I really loved about this day was the party afterward. There was a big celebration at our house. All of our family and friends came over for a huge party. We kids overindulged on sweets and played with cousins we didn't get to see often, and the adults enjoyed Uncle Pio's band, ate good food, and caught up with old friends and family members. The party went late into the night, and nobody noticed that my siblings and I stayed up way too late as well, arguing with other kids about the rules of a game. After that night, we promptly forgot the baptism at the center of it all as we started looking forward to our next family celebration, whatever that might be.

Every once in a while, I recall my brother's and sister's baptisms. I don't remember it because of the significance of the event itself but because my mother, who died when I was a teenager, appears in all the photographs from that day. She's dressed up and looks content and unconcerned. At this point in our family story, there were no plans to migrate anywhere. My mother looks happily settled in her home country. Because

I lost her when I was so young, each picture of her is a tiny resurrection. Each photograph is a way for me to know her outside of my memories, which are often tinged with sadness at losing her.

When I look at those photographs, I am also struck by the fact that Spanish saturated my life in those days. English was only a class at school that had no connection to my home. The priest performed the baptism in Spanish, and we all spoke Spanish at the party afterward. My schooling, my conversations, and my prayers were all strictly in Spanish for the first nine and a half years of my life. Little did I know that in just a few short years, my life would be immersed in English.

They are evangelicals!

I first learned to read in Spanish at the Catholic school I attended. Every day my brother and I would ride off on the school bus in the early morning, wearing our crisp uniforms. Our school offered an English class once a week, but somehow all I remember from those lessons is repeating in unison with my classmates, "Good morning, Miss Magaly!" Because it was a Catholic school, our teachers and administrators were also in charge of our religious education; some of them were nuns. Maybe I was too young or too distracted, but I remember little of my early Christian education. I do have vague memories of praying the Lord's Prayer, the Padre Nuestro. And I remember going to confession.

Prayer seemed to be the means some of the adults around me used to get to God. But I did not understand most of the words in the prayers. The language was far too sophisticated for me. I could recite them all by heart, but I could not explain the meaning of the words. Later, after we had moved to the United States, I had a similar experience when I learned to recite the Pledge of Allegiance in elementary school. I would stand up, place my hand over my heart, and say words like *allegiance* and *indivisible*. But I had no idea what any of it meant. With regard to prayer, all this confusion led me to the conclusion that God was remote and formal. God seemed to require religious jargon I did not really understand. So I was not very interested.

But I was intrigued by a church where my tío Pio, my mother's younger brother, sometimes took me. Growing up in a house in which everyone was always coming or going, I felt special to get one-on-one attention from my cool teenage uncle. We rode a bus across town to a building that looked nothing like a church. It looked like a store, and it was painted bright pink. The sign over the door indicated it was a church, but it wasn't named after a saint. These days, whenever I walk through my Latinx neighborhood in Baltimore and past small storefront churches called Vida Abundante (Abundant Life) or Solo por Gracia (Only by Grace), I think about my tío Pio's church.

Inside the church there were no pews, no incense, no crucifixes, and no statues of white saints in flowing robes. At that time I did not know what an evangelical church was. I only knew that my mother would sometimes point to women on the street who had long hair, wore no makeup, and donned loose, long dresses. She would whisper confidentially to me, "¡Ellas son evangélicas!" (They are evangelicals!). Evangelicalism sounded like a disease I did not want to catch. Not until later would I learn that Guatemalan evangelicals, at that time, dressed and acted differently to distinguish themselves from the rest of society.

But on those Sunday mornings, my uncle would walk me to a room full of kids sitting on a carpet on the floor. Then he'd leave to join the adults for worship. The teachers used puppets to teach the lesson by having the puppets ask questions and invite discussion. Then we prayed to God as if we were talking to each other, without kneeling or putting our hands together. I don't remember much else about what we did, but I remember that I learned at a very young age that there were different ways to connect with God. I had watched people in the Catholic Church experience intimacy with God while they lit candles and recited prayers with their rosaries. Now I had a glimpse of people whose faith could be taught through puppets and who prayed as if they were talking respectfully to another person.

In particular, I was struck by seeing adults and teenagers *choose* to be baptized! I didn't exactly understand why the evangelicals only baptized older people, not babies, or why they dunked them in a pool. But the event itself was something familiar to me. Baptism, as it turns out, is the one sacrament shared across all Christian traditions. It is the sacrament that affirms that we are buried with Christ and raised with him, as Paul writes in Colossians 2:12. In some churches, including Roman Catholic ones, baptism represents the grace of God's salvation that extends to the smallest child as they're initiated into the faith by their parents. For other churches, like my uncle's, baptism represents the costly decision to follow Jesus and to be united to a community of faith. Whether I recognized it or not, the experiences in that storefront church and in my Catholic parish shaped me and expanded my view of God.

We only went to that church a few times, because it was far from our house. I suspect my uncle didn't have as much fun as I did and that he was simply trying desperately to please his evangelical mother. I missed going to church with him because of the church itself and because I liked spending time with him. The experiences I had in that little storefront church are engraved in my memory just as much as family vacations, Christmas bikes, and piñatas at my birthday parties.

The country of the eternal spring

While in middle school in the United States, I once played a trick on a naive American classmate who asked me what kind of clothes people wore in Guatemala. It was as if he thought we were aliens on a distant planet. I was indignant and rolled my eyes, a gesture he didn't catch. So I told him that we didn't wear clothes in Guatemala. Everyone was naked all the time, I told him, because it was easier when we swung from vine to vine to get around town.

His eyes widened, which only encouraged me to embellish all the more. The first clothes I had ever worn we had bought at the airport right before we left for the United States, I told him. He nodded, a shocked expression on his face, and replied gravely, "I bet you were really glad to move here!"

The truth is that I wasn't. Our life in Guatemala was good. It was home. It was beautiful. When I was a little girl, I loved looking through family photo albums. Once I came across a picture of my parents before they had kids. They had ridden a motorcycle to a picturesque town and had been photographed in front of a pristine alpine lake. Surrounded by volcanoes and mountains, Lake Atitlán shines in the background. My mom's hair is windblown, and my dad has a scruffy beard. They look a little unkempt in their denim jackets, but they also look content and free. Whenever we visited this town, which was later discovered by American hippies and European tourists, my parents reminded us that they came here, to Panajachel, on their honeymoon.

When they would take our family there, my parents would hire any one of a dozen young men to take us around Lake Atitlán on their rickety boats and visit a few of the villages surrounding it. All the villages there were named after Jesus' twelve apostles and had distinct traditional dress. Walking the streets, you'd see women of all ages weaving colorful fabrics for their clothing or to sell to the many tourists. In a village called San Marcos La Laguna, we'd have dinner in an open-air restaurant overlooking the lake. There we would eat delicious Guatemalan food and look around the restaurant, wondering aloud if the American and European hippies were enjoying it as much as we were. In my more vulnerable moments, I wish I could return to days like this—days within my Guatemalan childhood. In those days I seemed to have had all the confidence in the world.

One such moment is the day I decided to attend literacy classes with our live-in housekeeper and nanny, Flavia. Flavia was from a town in the Guatemalan highlands called Tecpán and wore the traditional woven clothing from her village. Though she spoke both Spanish and Kaqchiquel, an indigenous language, she hadn't had the opportunity to go to school consistently. So although she was eighteen, she had never learned to read well. Now, my father informed her, literacy classes would be offered in the neighborhood. He strongly encouraged her to go, telling her she was welcome to take a few hours off work every week to attend classes.

At dinner one night, Flavia announced with enthusiasm that she would go to class as soon as the dishes were washed and put away. I'm not sure if she was giddy at the prospect of learning to read and write or just at the idea of getting away for an evening.

"Why are you going to classes?" I asked. I didn't know any adults who went to classes, and I was intrigued by whatever would be taught to adults. Maybe some secret lesson about what to do after kids go to sleep?

"I didn't learn to read and write very well, so I have to take more classes," she said as she cleared dishes.

"Like me!" I said. "I can't learn my eight times table, so the teacher said I have to practice it over and over until I know it by heart."

She nodded. "Yes, just like that."

"Maybe I should go with you, so I can learn my times tables," I added hopefully. Ever the extrovert, I was always looking for opportunities to be around people.

"Bueno," she said. At the time, it didn't occur to me that she was likely nervous about attending classes and probably only agreed to let me tag along so she wouldn't have to go alone.

That evening in class, the teacher asked everyone why he or she was there. I was the only kid in the room, and when she called on me, I said with all the bravado and naivete of a seven-year-old, “I’m here to learn my eight times table. Flavia told me that you help people learn things, and that’s what I have to learn.” The teacher gave me that smile adults like to give to kids, warm, knowing, and a little bit condescending.

Afterward, Flavia and I walked hand in hand back home. We stopped by the store and bought candy for two cents, and she let me practice those times tables all the way home.

When we first moved to the United States, two years after that saunter in the neighborhood with Flavia, we arrived at my tía Evelyn’s house in Rhode Island. She had a framed poster in her dining room, among the family pictures. It was a picture of Miss Guatemala from sometime in the 1970s, a woman who clearly had European ancestry, even as she was dressed in indigenous Guatemalan clothing with its signature colorful woven fabrics. She looked nothing like Flavia, whose tan skin complemented her clothing perfectly. But just below her feet were the words “Guatemala: The Country of the Eternal Spring.”

That’s how those class days with Flavia and my family felt: like an eternal spring, full of possibility and life; full of temperate days and something that felt like hope. This was our country.

Baptism revisited

When I was a young college student, I watched as people in my evangelical church got baptized. Each baptism I observed was a reminder that my own infant baptism couldn't have been that meaningful to me as a six-month-old. I didn't discuss this much with my new evangelical Christian friends, because I didn't want people to disparage the Catholic Church. I had sometimes heard people say that Catholics weren't real Christians—that they worship saints and memorize meaningless prayers—and I didn't want to hear more of it. I knew that was not true, but I did not know what *was* true. All I knew was that I felt protective of Catholicism, which was my first home in the faith. It signified more than faith for me. Catholicism was family; it was Guatemala. And it was an ancient church out of which the Protestant church emerged. But I would sometimes wonder: What did it mean to be baptized if my parents weren't Christians and had no intention of raising me in the faith?

I have a special fondness and gratitude for the Catholic Church. Even if my parents didn't intend to initiate me into the church out of devotion, it was the beginning of my journey with God. I didn't know God then, but God knew me. The Catholic culture of my family and Guatemala was significant in ways I can't articulate. Although I had little understanding of this sacred initiation into the church, the body of Christ, it was a beginning. Baptism set me on the path toward knowing God.

3

Abraham

The Immigrant Father of Our Faith

When a famine struck the land, Abram went down toward Egypt to live as an immigrant since the famine was so severe in the land.

—**GENESIS 12:10**

Francisco Barrera spent a summer evening celebrating a friend's birthday. Like many people in such situations, he drank a lot at the party, which was held at a female friend's house near Washington, D.C. Realizing that he should not drive home in his inebriated state but also that he shouldn't stay overnight at his friend's house, he opted to sleep in his car. It was three in the morning, so it would be daylight in a few hours. He would be sober by then and able to drive home safely. So he put his car keys in his pocket, reclined the driver's seat, and promptly dozed off.

Francisco was woken up by knocking at his window and the glare of a bright flashlight in his eyes. He could see the police lights behind his car, and an officer asked him to roll down his window. He did so, wondering what was happening and what he had done wrong. Francisco did not speak much English, but he knew it was important to do whatever the officer asked. He was told to breathe into an instrument, and then the officer asked him to step out of the car, where he was arrested and charged with driving under the influence. Francisco did not know that in Maryland, sitting in the driver's seat while inebriated can result in a DUI charge. Even if the car is turned off. Even if the keys are not in the ignition.

His car was impounded, and somehow Immigration and Customs Enforcement (ICE) learned of his arrest. Francisco was an undocumented immigrant, even though his wife and two children were U.S. citizens. ICE officials put him in deportation proceedings. A competent immigration lawyer pleaded his case in immigration court, emphasizing that Francisco had always been a hard worker and had never been in trouble with the law. But the federal judge decided his DUI made him an undesirable criminal immigrant. So Francisco was deported and separated from his family.

I never met Francisco Barrera, but when I started working in the immigration legal clinic at World Relief, a colleague told me about his case. My work with World Relief would be to engage Baltimore churches in learning a biblical view of immigrants and immigration, so I wanted to learn some recent stories. I had heard our immigration system needed reform, but I was stunned when I reviewed Francisco's file and heard his story—so much so that when I met friends for dinner that evening, I related the whole story to them. "That's like arresting the good Samaritan for kidnapping!" one of them retorted. "The man was trying to be a good neighbor by not driving drunk." Other people who have heard the same story have countered that Francisco broke the law, even if he did not know it was a law, and was rightly deported. Many say that he had already broken the law by crossing the border illegally, so he should have never been here in the first place to get that questionable DUI.

But if Francisco Barrera is a criminal immigrant, so is one of the heroes of our faith. It may be uncomfortable for us to reflect on the fact that a great father of our faith could be considered a criminal immigrant. But as we look at the stories of immigrants in Scripture, this is a reality with which we must reckon.

Abraham, the criminal immigrant

Abraham: most of us are not accustomed to thinking of him as an immigrant, let alone a criminal one. Yet Genesis introduces us to Abram (whose name will change to Abraham after God makes a covenant with him) just as the Lord is asking him to migrate to the land of Canaan (Genesis 12:1). It takes just a few verses for the nomadic Abram to find himself amid a famine, which drives him to migrate yet again to find sustenance in what would become the preferred destination for the hungry: Egypt.

The climate in the ancient world of the Near East fluctuated greatly thanks to its location between the Mediterranean Sea to the west and the Arabian Desert to the east. The semiarid land was unpredictable for the people who depended on it to produce, as the nomads who fill the pages of Genesis did. But ancient Egypt had no such problems. The Nile and its fertile delta and riverbanks provided abundantly for inhabitants and drew small bands of immigrants like Abram and his family.[1]

Out of fear, Abram presents Sarai, his wife—later known as Sarah—as his sister when they arrive in Egypt. She is beautiful and, apparently, desirable even at her sixty-five years of age. This fact becomes a liability for Abraham.[2] Believing the Egyptians will kill him in order to have her, he acts in a way most of us would consider cowardly. He acts out of self-interest, using her to protect himself. "So tell them you are my sister so that they will treat me well for your sake, and I will survive because of you," he says (Genesis 12:13). Abram prefers to sacrifice Sarai's well-being rather than suffer himself. And indeed, while Sarai is sent to the pharaoh's household, Abram prospers: "Things went well for Abram because of her: he acquired flocks, cattle, male donkeys, men servants, women servants, female donkeys, and camels" (Genesis 12:16).

In modern terms, we could say that Abraham traffics his wife. He receives payment and grows wealthy from her sexual exploitation. He commits fraud by presenting her as his sister, a convenient half-truth, and he coerces her into a situation with no way out. This is the very definition of human trafficking.[3]

Sarai has no voice in this matter. In this way, she is doubly displaced: first as an immigrant and then as a victim of human trafficking. Notably, this will not be the last time Abram traffics his wife. In Genesis 20, after God has made a covenant with him and changed his name, Abraham enters the territory of Abimelech, king of the Philistines, and repeats these actions. Thanks to God's intervention and protection in the latter incident, Sarah is saved from having to spend a single night with the king.

Without protection, without connection

As Christians, we make allowances for the crimes of Abraham because we have listened to his full story. Reading this story in the Bible, most Christians forgive Abraham for these transgressions. Most of us understand their placement within his larger story with God. We assume that this kind of thing must have happened all the time in the ancient Near East. Yes, Abraham may have made mistakes, but he is still the father of our Judeo-Christian faith, and is cited as a prime example of faith in the New Testament. The author of Hebrews counts Abraham among the heroes of the faith: "By faith Abraham obeyed when he was called to go out to a place that he was going to receive as an inheritance" (Hebrews 11:8). We know he broke the law, but we also listen to the specifics of his story and the mitigating circumstances that brought him to such terrible actions.

Yet many of us don't extend that same consideration to unauthorized immigrants whose crime is crossing the U.S.-Mexico border, a criminal misdemeanor. The parallel is remarkable: many of the arrivals at the border also fear for their lives and simply want to survive. Rabbi Maurice Harris notes that Abraham lies in order to survive in a foreign nation where he is not welcome. "It must have been agonizing," writes Harris. "It's a story of strangers in a strange land, without protection, without connections and without a right to go about their business unmolested. It's an illegal immigrant's story."[4]

I have sat with immigrants and taken down their stories for affidavits attached to immigration petitions. In those conversations, many speak with regret about having had to break the law. They had tried to do things the right way, often several times. But their visa application was rejected, or they were told when they applied for asylum that they hadn't proven a credible fear of persecution. So in desperation, many of them endured a perilous journey and did whatever they had to do to survive. Sometimes this included breaking the law by crossing the border and making a home for themselves in the United States. Women often tell their stories through tears, reluctant to speak of the sexual assault they experienced along the way. According to Amnesty International, more than 60 percent of immigrant women crossing the border into the United States are sexually assaulted.[5]

Like Sarah, immigrant women are even more vulnerable to human trafficking than women who are not immigrants.[6] It's difficult to find accurate information on trafficking, but some organizations have said that as many as 80 percent of trafficking victims are foreign-born women and girls. It's not uncommon to hear stories of women working in appalling conditions, under lock and key without a day of rest, while also experiencing sexual abuse.

Abraham does not have the permission of the authorities to enter Egypt. Later he moves into the land of the Philistines, also without authorization. But he and Sarah seek only to find sustenance and a livelihood. They do no harm to the people upon whose land they have trespassed.

It's tempting to conclude that if immigrants broke the law by crossing the border, they must be more prone to criminality—that we must be suspicious of them because they pose a danger to citizens. But one hundred years of research on the link between immigration and criminal behavior reveals that conclusion to be false. Research has shown, over and over again, that immigration is associated with lower rates of violent and property crime. Immigrants are actually less likely than the native-born to commit serious crimes or be imprisoned.[7]

Laws of nation, laws of God

None of this means that laws are not important or should be broken at will. When we find ourselves in situations we would rather escape, breaking the law should not be our first impulse. As a Christian and a student of the Bible, I have read the sacred law of the Hebrew Scriptures given to God's people. God's law consists of instructions for everyday life and worship while also giving direct guidance on how to form a just society. I also know that many of the laws given in the U.S. Constitution were intended by the founding fathers to protect the republic they sought to build.

I believe in laws. I also know that when we follow Christ, our first allegiance must be to him. For Christians, allegiance to any nation is secondary. When we are part of the kingdom of God, our first loyalty is to a "nation" that covers the entire globe and knows no borders. As the apostle Paul reminds the Christians in the Philippian church who lived under Roman rule, "Our citizenship is in heaven. We look forward to a savior that comes from there—the Lord Jesus Christ" (Philippians 3:20).

As much as I believe in laws, I also wonder if we often value our human-made laws more than the human beings that they were designed to guide or protect. The immigration laws of Canada or the United States or China or Germany are not God's immutable laws. The United States is a constitutional republic whose laws change all the time because citizens recognize that the law is not inerrant. At one time in U.S. history, it was legal to own people as property. It was also legal to count an African brought here in chains as three-fifths of a person. It was legal to deny women the right to vote and own property. People eventually recognized these laws were unjust, and they were amended. Some were rightly repealed altogether.

Just as we set Abraham's transgressions within the context of his larger story, we must also listen to the stories that immigrants are telling us. As followers of Jesus, we respond to a higher law than that of nations. We also know that good laws are organic, not static. They respond to people and their unique vulnerabilities. They resist harming people who get caught up by forces beyond their control—forces that put them in the position of taking terrible and dangerous risks to try to help themselves and their families survive. Dr. Martin Luther King put it this way, describing the higher law the good Samaritan obeyed:

> Man-made laws assure justice, but a higher law produces love. No code of conduct ever persuaded a father to love his children or a husband to show affection to his wife. The law court may force him to provide bread for the family,

> but it cannot make him provide the bread of love. A good father is obedient to the unenforceable. The good Samaritan represents the conscience of mankind because he also was obedient to that which could not be enforced. No law in the world could have produced such unalloyed compassion, such genuine love, such thorough altruism.[8]

Amending the laws of an outdated immigration system is not beyond our reach. We have the ability to elect leaders and influence legislation, and as Christians, we should. As followers of Jesus, we are to be "obedient to the unenforceable": devoted to the higher calling of Christ, which goes beyond the law of the land.

Jesus is at the border answering the question asked of him by a religious legal expert in Luke 10:29: "And who is my neighbor?" Your neighbor is the Mexican, Honduran, Salvadoran, and Guatemalan immigrant in need. Indeed, those of every nationality are our neighbors.

Immigration laws cannot love our immigrant neighbors; only we, people, can do that. Laws can, however, protect immigrants from falling prey to those who see their vulnerability and seek to take advantage by victimizing them. As King went on to say: "Judicial decrees cannot change the heart, but they can restrain the heartless. . . . The habits, if not the hearts, of people have been and are being altered every day by legislative acts, judicial decisions, and executive orders."[9]

Punitive immigration laws

That first week I worked at World Relief, I learned that Francisco had crossed the border unlawfully because there were no opportunities in his country. Faced with a bleak future, little education, and no way to make a life for himself, he crossed the border with the help of a *coyote*, or human smuggler. A few years later, when he met and married his U.S. citizen wife, they had hoped he would be able to adjust his status through her sponsorship. But in the 1990s an immigration statute called "the three- and ten-year bars" was added to U.S. immigration laws.[10] It states that any immigrant who wasn't lawfully admitted to the United States and acquired more than six months or one year of unlawful presence is barred from adjusting their status unless they leave the United States for three or ten years, respectively. This statute was intended to deter unlawful immigration. But because so few immigrants even knew of its existence, it failed to do its job.

By the time he learned of this provision in the law, Francisco was already a father of two, including a child with special needs, and was the sole supporter of his family. He couldn't return to Mexico and provide for his family, so he opted to stay while he and his wife hoped and prayed he would remain undetected by ICE. His wife was devastated by his arrest; she and Francisco turned their hopes toward the immigration attorney who would fight for them, and the federal judge who would hear Francisco's case. Few people understand how discretionary immigration laws are—a judge is free to decide the case without guidelines or the consideration of precedents. Francisco's fate rested on the judge alone.

For reasons known only to the judge himself, he chose to deport Francisco. Having lost their provider, his wife and children turned to public benefits for their survival and reluctantly adjusted to life without their husband and father. This is the punitive effect of current U.S. immigration laws—a person who might otherwise have qualified for permanent residence is instead deported, and a family that would have remained together is torn apart, with some members going on public assistance.

Laws failed to care for Francisco and his family. And when I consider the situation in which Sarah and Abraham found themselves, I wonder how laws might have provided protection and care for them too. Just as Francisco was seeking a better life, Sarah and Abraham were nomads. They were simply obeying their God as faithfully as they could and seeking survival for themselves and their household.

What went through Sarah's mind as she was used and abused? Did she question whether this was the only way that Abraham could be safe and prosper? Did she wonder if the God who had called them out of their homeland saw her suffering and would answer? I imagine that she cried out to her God every day, hoping for mercy and a reunion with her husband.

I also like to think she encountered God in her imprisonment in those lands. Scripture is rife with narratives of those whom the world discards and devalues but whom God sees and remembers. Sarah must have known that God saw her in her affliction, just as Abraham knew that God saw him in his transgression. Ultimately, God rescued both of them out of these terrible situations, keeping the promise to bless them and their descendants.

4

Communion

Isn't the cup of blessing that we bless a sharing in the blood of Christ? Isn't the loaf of bread that we break a sharing in the body of Christ?

—1 CORINTHIANS 10:16

The first time I participated in the sacrament of communion I was nine years old. I did not understand a single thing about the eucharist, but I was too intimidated to ask questions. Those emotions—confusion, intimidation, bewilderment—became emblematic of my entire life of faith until I became an adult.

The event itself wasn't just one day—it was the culmination of what seemed to me like hundreds of days. My friend Juanjo and I took classes every week at the Catholic church of Santo Domingo, our neighborhood parish. Initially, about ten kids from our neighborhood went to classes together, but gradually everyone except Juanjo and me dropped out. It was more fun to play kickball and other games than to walk all the way to the Catholic church to take classes. So one day it was just Juanjo and me, heading to class together. Taking all those classes in preparation for my first communion was reminiscent of waiting for my birthday or Christmas. It felt like an eternity.

I don't remember any of these classes, but I know that I distinctly chose to pursue my first communion. The church requirement was that all kids were to have the knowledge and preparation needed to understand communion as a sacrament and to receive the body and blood of Christ with devotion. On the day of my first communion, I had no such understanding. But I went through with it anyway, because I wanted to wear my pretty white dress and know God. I didn't know how one gets to God except by being good and participating in the life of the church. Communion, it seemed to me, was an extremely important part of the life of faith and might help me find some peace and security amid my increasingly turbulent world.

My feelings at the time were complicated. I mostly felt untethered and fearful, although I did not have the words to express these emotions. Guatemala at that time was in the midst of a bloody civil war that claimed the lives of more than two hundred thousand people.[1] It was a war that began in 1960 and concluded thirty-six years later, in 1996. In seminary I would learn that a large urban population of Guatemalans outside Guatemala City was in Los Angeles—made up of many people who fled during that time so they wouldn't become the casualties of that war.

My father had already left for the United States, and we had not seen him in almost a year. He left partly because, as a self-proclaimed socialist, he was in danger. In the political situation in Guatemala in the early 1980s, he might have been considered a dissident. But he also left because the political turmoil had destabilized the Guatemalan economy. Jobs were few and difficult to get without the right connections. He moved to Rhode Island, where his own mother and siblings lived, and he sent us money and letters. In those letters he made drawings of each of us and encouraged us to be good and to listen to our mother.

But I wasn't reassured by his letters. I had overheard the hushed conversations between my parents and their friends before my father left—whispers about people who had "disappeared." Some of these were people they worked with or had gone to school with. Even at eight years old, I knew that might have been my father's fate as well if he hadn't chosen to leave.

Along with my father's leaving came the announcement that my family couldn't afford to send me to Catholic school anymore. I would now have to go to the public school. In fact, we were struggling so much financially that we would have to borrow my communion dress, veil, gloves, and all the other regalia from our neighbor across the street: my friend Ana Cecilia, whose mother had graciously offered the use of her dress.

Ana Cecilia's mom and my mom were friendly and often chatted casually. It was at Ana Cecilia's house that I overheard my mother say that she wasn't excited about my sudden interest in religion but that she wouldn't prevent me from pursuing faith either. She added that she was happy that I was at least staying out of trouble and spending afternoons in church. But it was clear that she couldn't figure out why I was so committed to exploring the faith that she and my father had abandoned.

Once I had everything I needed to participate in the ceremony, I was ready. In my borrowed dress, I held a candle and a little prayer book in my gloved hands. I knelt in front of the priest and took communion for the first time. I don't remember if I felt closer to God at that moment, but I knew this was an important step. Surely now God would help me to figure out how to pursue a life of faith, I thought.

But my communion preparation classes were entirely disconnected from my lived reality. What did it mean to drink a tiny bit of wine and eat a tasteless wafer? How could wine and bread matter in light of everything happening around me?

The man in the creek

When I was in high school, my American history teacher invited four Vietnam veterans to our class to talk about their experiences in the war. They were all men about my father's age, and some were fathers of students in the class. One of them talked about the shock of seeing a dead body for the first time and how that experience changed him.

Seeing me in that classroom along with my classmates, most of whom were white, our veteran guests couldn't have known that I had seen my own share of dead bodies in Guatemala. They discussed a different war with different objectives. But the result was the same: lots of innocent people died. While I was not a combat veteran, I identified with some of their experiences. But I did not say so; I didn't want to let it be known that I was any different from the rest of my classmates, who had only seen make-believe deaths in war movies and on TV shows.

One day when I was about seven years old, I was playing outside with kids from the neighborhood. Someone must have suggested we go for a walk. None of us were supposed to leave our street. But as most children do at some point, we decided to push the boundaries. We yearned to explore beyond the familiar parts of the neighborhood, so we walked a few streets over to a road that ran along a ravine. It seemed like miles to me, because I had never wandered that far away without an adult, but it was probably only a few blocks.

When we reached the end of the street, it turned into a dirt path that became smaller and smaller. I was afraid but determined to be brave in front of my brother and all our friends, so I climbed down the embankment after everyone else and sat on a mound of dirt. As usual, I was the one in the group who couldn't keep up with all the other kids. I had scarcely caught my breath when everyone began to gather around something near the creek.

I caught up to find out what everyone was looking at. It was a dead body—the body of a man with a mustache. The corpse looked blue to me and had lots of marks all over his body. The water in the creek trickled by as we stared at the man in disbelief. One boy poked the body with a stick. Another said that he must have drowned. Somebody noted that people who drown don't have those marks all over their body. I didn't know it at the time, but those marks revealed he had been tortured.

I don't even remember how I got home from there, but only that I was in a hurry to get away. I desperately wanted to ask my parents about it, but then I'd have to reveal that I had been somewhere I wasn't supposed to be. So I prayed that I could forget about that terrible scene and not be afraid. That scene became the stuff of my nightmares.

I started to recite all the prayers I'd learned by heart at church and in school. But faith did not come easily to me. By nature, I was a willful and pessimistic child, and that obstinacy extended to my attempts to reach God. Some days I tried desperately to believe in God as an antidote to my fears about the dead man. Other days I felt foolish for even trying to talk to God, certain that I was speaking words that faded with my breath and didn't reach even my sleeping brother in the same room.

Now that I work for an organization that serves in conflict transformation and disaster relief, I often wonder how parents explain to young children what war is and why they're forced to leave their homes. My parents gave me no such explanation, likely believing that I wasn't aware of the rumblings of war and unrest. But of course I was. In those months, I lay awake night after night, sleepless with fear and anxiety. I tried to reassure myself that the man must have done something very bad and that was why he was dead. If he deserved it, then I didn't have to be afraid.

Most of the people killed during those years were indigenous, like Flavia, who had taken care of my siblings and me for so many years. Indigenous people were raped; they were tortured; they were kidnapped; and they were murdered systematically by our own Guatemalan government. Entire villages were slaughtered. People were "disappeared." And so many were displaced that some chose to leave their home country to make a new life in a safer place.

A war funded by the United States

Most troubling was the day I learned that this war was largely funded by the United States. Some people find it curious that I didn't learn this information until after I had moved to the United States with my family. This information is now widely known and affirmed, but at the time, it was novel and astonishing.

I'm old enough to remember the Cold War and the threat of communism getting a foothold in the Americas after the revolution in Cuba. I was a high school senior when the Berlin Wall was torn down and the entire Western world rejoiced at the collapse of the Soviet Union. What I didn't know then is that the foreign policy of the United States included funding military dictatorships in Guatemala and other nations in Latin America to quell leftist guerrilla warfare that rose up in response to human rights abuses. U.S. leaders did not care what happened to our people as long as communism didn't spread anywhere near their borders.

The day I found out that the Guatemalan war, which we had fled, was funded by the government of the country to which we had moved, I was furious. The United States was my home now; sometimes I would tell people that while Guatemala was my mother country, I'd been joyfully adopted by my uncle Sam! I believed the words in the Pledge of Allegiance that said this was a country of liberty and justice for all. When I learned that arms had been secretly shipped to the Guatemalan government for years, for the purpose of squashing socialist uprisings—many of which demanded a fair distribution of land and rights for the indigenous population—well, I felt disillusioned and betrayed. The anger at that injustice formed in my belly like a fire, and it grew. I was determined to do something about it, but my reach was limited because I was in high school.

In my somewhat misguided zeal for justice, I announced to my homeroom teacher, Mrs. Babcock, that I would no longer be reciting or standing for the Pledge of Allegiance. I pulled an article from the *St. Petersburg Times* editorial page out of my pocket and handed the crumpled mess to her. Surely she would accept my act of civil disobedience when she read about the United States' foreign policy in Guatemala.

Mrs. Babcock didn't see things my way. Now, having been a teacher myself, I'm not surprised. The last thing any teacher wants is an act of rebellion in a room of students she needs to keep in order! At the time, however, I couldn't believe it, and I didn't keep quiet. She was the one who taught us about Dr. King and Henry David Thoreau! Defiantly, I sat down and said, "I have a right to protest the U.S. government. They are responsible for the deaths of hundreds of thousands of Guatemalans, and I am a Guatemalan!"

Mrs. Babcock was not backing down either. "Karen! You enjoy the benefits of living in this country, and you will stand up right now out of respect for it."

"No, I won't!" I crossed my arms and sat in my desk like it was my job.

Our standoff ended with a visit to the assistant principal's office and my reluctant agreement to stand during the pledge but not recite it. I assured my teacher and my assistant principal that this was *not* a concession to their demand that I respect the pledge. I would stand, but I would be silent in protest, I reminded them. Then I walked out with my head held high and headed to my next class.

The eucharist revisited

During seminary, when I lived in California, I once made a joking toast while hanging out with friends. "To Ronald Reagan," I said, as I raised my glass. "Had he not funded a civil war in my country, my family would have never left Guatemala and I would have never met all you fine people!"

Today, I can scarcely believe I would say something that flippant about the painful displacement of my family. Just like my family, most immigrants never dream of leaving their countries. In fact, when we leave, we leave pieces of ourselves behind. We leave our homes, our comforts, our heart languages, our extended or immediate families, and our sense of self. We have to start all over again, almost like children, in a new country.

It used to shock me that so many Christians I knew loved Ronald Reagan and thought him a leader who pursued policies that furthered the interests of Christians. Even in high school, when the subject came up, I would sometimes let people know about foreign policy in Latin America under Reagan. They seemed to like me, but their generosity of heart didn't seem to extend to the Guatemalans they did *not* know.

In another high school class during my senior year, one of my teachers, Mr. Stewart, took a group of us to see a film called *Romero*, the true story of slain Archbishop Óscar Romero in El Salvador. El Salvador is Guatemala's immediate neighbor and suffered the same fate as Guatemala in regard to U.S. foreign policy. In the film, the quiet, bookish Romero gradually transforms into the most outspoken voice against the U.S.-funded death squads in his country. At that time, U.S. political leaders affirmed that human rights abuses in Central America were unfortunate, but the groups that supported the poor were communist, and communism could not be tolerated in the Americas. Because Monseñor Romero was firmly on the side of the poor and the oppressed, his own government targeted him for death.

The most troubling aspect of the film by far is its accurate depiction of his assassination. Each week during his nationally broadcast homily, Monseñor Romero would say the names of those who had been killed. This act of remembrance cost him his life. He reminded his government that those who had been murdered were witnesses to the violent repression and would not be forgotten. One day, while the archbishop celebrated the eucharist, a gunman stormed into the back of the church. A single shot rang out, and Monseñor Romero—who had just raised the chalice of wine, the blood of Christ, to bless it—was struck; a bullet pierced his heart. The chalice fell from his hands as Romero himself fell. In the movie, the wine spilling all over his white priestly vestments was indistinguishable from the blood pouring from his own chest.

I remember watching this poignant scene and crying in the theater. I am normally a highly verbal person who processes movies out loud right after they're over, but I was struck with silence as the credits rolled. Archbishop Romero saw the work of liberating the people of El Salvador, people suffering just like their Guatemalan neighbors, as a natural extension of his faith, and he paid the ultimate price for it.

Romero's words and witness still hold truth today. "A church that does not provoke crisis, a gospel that does not disturb, a word of God that does not rankle, a word of God that does not touch the concrete sin of the society in which it is being proclaimed—what kind of gospel is that? Just nice pious considerations that bother nobody."[2]

Learning about Romero's life and work taught me that the gospel has implications beyond personal piety. But that doesn't mean we abandon worship, devotion, and the sacraments. Even at crisis moments in his country, Romero was gathering his people to partake in the sacred meal of the eucharist and remember both the suffering of Christ and the suffering of his people.

In many Christian traditions, when we take communion we remember Christ suffered, died, rose from the dead, and will return. For many of us Protestants, it's an important metaphorical act of remembrance. In contrast, Roman Catholics believe in transubstantiation: that the bread and wine, when consecrated, become the actual body and blood of Christ. In this view, the essence of the bread and wine are completely changed into the body and blood of Christ. How this happens exactly is a mystery but a reality, nonetheless. All of this means that, according to Catholic tradition, Romero was with Christ when he died, holding his very blood.

So what could that small wafer and that sip of wine at my first communion mean to me in the midst of the war-torn country of my childhood? How could they possibly matter? The eucharist was exactly what I needed, although I didn't know it. I needed the presence of Christ, the Prince of Peace, amid my turmoil and my country's crises.

As Jesus celebrated the Last Supper, he knew he would face the cross of Calvary the very next day. When we take communion, we share in the suffering of Christ and in his presence. As we suffer with Christ, we come into union with him. I may not have fully understood what was happening at my first communion, but the Holy Spirit, the great Comforter, was present with me. There is a resonance in communion for those who suffer and seek liberation.

These days, I embrace the eucharist as a mystery of faith. It helps me identify and share with Christ and his suffering. As I think about the plight of refugees and immigrants, not just in the United States but around the world, I know that Christ suffers with them. When I take communion now, kneeling at the front of my Lutheran church, I remember that I serve a God who knew pain. I remember that I serve a Man of Sorrows—a suffering servant who sees immigrants and their suffering and remembers them.

5

Hagar

The "Foreign Thing" and the God Who Sees Her

Hagar named the Lord who spoke to her, "You are El Roi" because she said, "Can I still see after he saw me?"
—GENESIS 16:13

I taught English in the Central Asian Republic of Kazakhstan for two years. My Kazakh students had beautiful and deeply meaningful names. I had a student named Aslan (emphasis on the second syllable), which I found out means "lion" in Turkish. Other students had names that translated as "White Camel" or "Silk." It was a little awkward when people would ask me about my own name, assuming it held significance or a story. In fact, I'd only discovered the meaning of my name in a book of baby names when I was thirteen.

It's difficult for us to imagine a world in which someone is named "Foreign Thing." This was the case for Hagar, the slave of Sarai who became the mother of Ishmael. We do not know her true name. But in the biblical Hebrew she is referred to as *Hagar*, which translates approximately as "foreign thing."

As an immigrant, I can't imagine a situation more dehumanizing than being referred to as Foreign Thing. The very idea makes my blood boil. As one theologian has noted, "A name is not just a word by which one is identified. A name also provides the conceptual framework, the point of reference, the mental constructs that are used in thinking, understanding, and relating to a person."[1] A name is central to identity and humanity.

But Foreign Thing is the name given to Hagar when she enters the Hebrew Scriptures in Genesis 16. By then, she was already an enslaved person in Abram's household.

Hagar sees God

It's very likely that Hagar came to live with Abram and Sarai during their sojourn in Egypt. Depending on which translation of the Bible you are reading, she is described as Sarai's handmaiden, servant, slave, maidservant, or maid.

Hagar labored in their household even to the point of bearing a child who would not be considered hers but theirs. Even her own body and her offspring are not considered her own. Although the practice of giving a servant to a husband to bear a child is unheard of in our context, it was legal and not uncommon in the ancient Near East. But no sooner does Hagar become pregnant than her troubles worsen. The Scripture says she "disrespected" her mistress, so Sarai deals harshly with her; some theologians say Sarai oppresses her. A pregnant Hagar runs away to the desert, seeking her own liberation.

This is where her story takes an unexpected turn. Hagar becomes the first person in the Bible to receive an annunciation—an appearance, or special message, from God—and the first to give God a name. A messenger of God appears to her, urging her to return to her mistress and promising that she will bear many children. She is instructed to give the child in her womb the name Ishmael, meaning "God hears" (Genesis 16:11). It is noteworthy that her annunciation is nearly identical to Mary's in the Gospels. And when God's messenger has finished speaking to Hagar, she responds, "You are El Roi [the God who sees]" because, as verse 13 tells us, she said, "Can I still see after he saw me?"

Hagar had good reason for her surprise at having survived an encounter with God, writes theologian Megan McKenna. "Tradition said that if a person saw God, the person died from the encounter. And she gives God a name! The God of Vision—of far seeing, of the future, of knowing the present and taking note of her, just a maid, a pregnant slave, and an Egyptian, not even a Jew."[2]

As if that were not enough, Hagar meets God *again* in the desert, this time while fleeing Sarah's mistreatment and eviction from the household. Fearing the likely death of her young son, Hagar can't bear to watch him suffer. She places him under a bush and sits some distance away, crying out in grief and weeping.

Genesis 21:17-21 tells us,

> God heard the boy's cries, and God's messenger called to Hagar from heaven and said to her, "Hagar! What's wrong? Don't be afraid. God has heard the boy's cries over there. Get up, pick up the boy, and take him by the hand because I will make of him a great nation." Then God opened her eyes, and she saw a well. She went over, filled the water flask, and gave the boy a drink. God remained with the boy; he grew up, lived in the desert, and became an expert archer. He lived in the Paran desert, and his mother found him an Egyptian wife.

God sees and responds to Hagar's suffering a second time. She hears from God's messenger that, although Sarah may have tossed her and her son out like garbage, God is determined not only to save their lives but to bless them. She will get to watch her boy grow up and will see him marry from among her own people, the Egyptians. Unlike Sarah, who laughed at God's promises, Hagar responds to God's provision with open hands. She has a special understanding of God because God cared for her and Ishmael in the desert as a compassionate mother would have done. God cared for her deeply and tangibly regardless of the fact that she was an enslaved foreigner. And all this even though she did not bear the child of the promise to Abraham.

Tradition in Israel and in the Hebrew Scriptures is that there is no difference between God and messengers of God. God visits Hagar! Messengers of God sometimes appear to biblical characters—including, most famously, Mary, the mother of Jesus. But this messenger appears to an enslaved Egyptian girl, a "foreign thing" who belongs to Sarai to do with as she pleases, including mistreat or throw out.

Hagar in the desert reminds all of us that the Spirit can be found in the places we least expect: with the poor, the outcasts, the enslaved people, the domestic help, and the foreigners. God is present with anyone who is treated as a human resource instead of a human being. God shows up not just for the master and mistress of the house and the native citizens with rights but for the undocumented maid in the kitchen.

And who would have imagined that the undocumented maid didn't just bring needs—for refuge or economic opportunity? Who knew that she also brought gifts: faith and devotion, hard work, talents, rich cultural traditions, and a family that would grow up and integrate into the adopted country?

Lo cotidiano, the everyday

I've often wondered if my female relatives would have identified with Hagar had they been taught her story. Like many immigrants, my abuelita, my mother, and a few aunts have all worked as housekeepers in the informal U.S. economy. In Guatemala, some of them trained as nurses, bookkeepers, and teachers, but their education and skills required recertification at great cost or native fluency in English. So in the United States, many of them worked as maids in wealthy American households.

My mother's mother, my abuelita Amada, worked for nearly two decades as a live-in housekeeper and nanny for a wealthy family in Brentwood, an affluent neighborhood in Los Angeles. While housekeeping isn't a job anyone in the United States particularly dreams of doing, I remember how grateful my abuelita was for having work—especially as she was an unauthorized immigrant for most of the time she lived in the United States. "Vergüenza es robar" (It's shameful to steal), she would say, "but there is no shame in working hard."

And work hard she did. She cleaned, ordered, and organized an American home. She cared for children who were not her own while her employers pursued more lucrative work. My grandmother didn't mind this kind of work, because she understood something that for years I've struggled to understand: all work has meaning, and all work has dignity.

While washing dishes isn't glamorous or exciting work, it is necessary work in the world. And our God engaged in humble work just as we do—work that we might deem too lowly for the Creator of the universe. The Bible tells us in Genesis 1 that God takes chaos, darkness, and meaninglessness and orders the universe from them. God separates light, waters, and land, creating something out of nothing.

And then after six days of work, God leaves creation unfinished, intending for human beings to complete it. God tells the human beings that they are God's image-bearers. As such, they are to work for six days and rest for one day too.

My abuelita's work had meaning not because it produced clean linens and spotless floors. Her work meant something because it reflected the working God who created her. She bore God's image, and she recognized the image of God in those around her.

I imagine her there in that Los Angeles mansion, ordering that family's universe: sorting laundry like darkness and light, bringing order and routine to children's schedules, taking strange American ingredients and creating nourishing meals and healthy snacks, calling them into being. Theologian Ada María Isasi-Díaz refers to this outworking of faith as *lo cotidiano*: the everyday lived experiences of Latinas, the everyday struggle to survive.[3] This is how my abuelita lived her faith. Like Ruth and Naomi, she fought to survive and worked out her faith in the ordinary tasks of her days.

I have no way of knowing if the family that employed her ever truly saw my abuelita as an image-bearer of God, as someone God saw and remembered, as a theologian and the spiritual mother of her family. Nonetheless, it was true, just as it was true that Hagar reflected the image of God. My abuelita contributed more than hard work to her new country; she brought the gift of her faith, her theology of survival.

The claim that immigrants are God's image-bearers—human beings whose dignity and worth should be respected—may seem a political or even revolutionary statement. Just as Sarah forgot about her own mistreatment in Egypt and the land of the Philistines and turned around to oppress Hagar, many North Americans have a kind of convenient amnesia when it comes to their own immigrant past. Recently, a well-known news broadcaster was boasting, along with a picture of himself in Ireland, of his Irish heritage and his ancestors' legal migration. I will assume that he did not know that the date he posted as the year of their migration occurred several decades before there were any federal immigration laws. If there were no laws, then his family couldn't have migrated legally or illegally. Rather, they simply benefited from a country with an open door that welcomed those seeking a better life. I often hear Americans proudly discussing their immigrant heritage—while in the same breath wanting to shut the door on the immigrants coming to the United States today.

The implication seems to be that immigrants have changed. The truth is that immigrants are the same—they have the same need and the same humanity. It's the laws that have changed.

Shut the door behind me

Years ago, when I lived in Kazakhstan, I taught a class on conversational English through American culture topics. It was a fascinating class for my students, who discussed topics like how to play baseball ("strange game") and the wedding tradition of the bouquet toss ("Tell us why they throw the flowers!").

It was also in this class that I was introduced to a book about American culture that began with a history of the United States as a great nation built by immigrants. It described English pilgrims fleeing religious persecution, as well as Ellis Island and the many European immigrants who were processed there in the late nineteenth and early twentieth centuries. Then, on the same page, it declared that immigrants were no longer necessary in the United States. It had moved past the time when it needed immigrant populations to develop natural resources and populate the western part of the country. Immigrants, the book implied, were no longer a blessing; they were a burden.

You may be surprised that I became convinced by this argument, but I did. I had solid information—from a textbook, no less—and I felt as though I'd solved a math problem whose solution had eluded me for years. So even though I had immigrated to the United States from Guatemala as a child with my parents and siblings, I now adopted the position I'd heard proclaimed in many public spaces. Much like some political leaders have done—despite having parents who were immigrants—I arrived at the conclusion that the immigration door should be shut firmly behind my family and me.

That was the end of that, as far as I was concerned.

Like that younger self of mine, many people—whether native-born citizens or documented immigrants—become convinced by information that is incomplete or inaccurate. My own immigration success story was receding into the distant past; now that I had become a legal resident and then a naturalized citizen, I had few relationships with undocumented immigrants or refugees. In fact, by the time I arrived at the conclusion that immigrants were burdensome, the few immigrants, documented or not, whom I did know were mostly people in my family. I received the information in that book as cold, hard truth that must be enforced without mercy. Truth be told, it reinforced what I often heard on the news, in church circles, and even from some of my relatives. So it wasn't hard to accept as fact the idea that immigration was no longer good for the United States.

What I forgot during this period is that when we talk about immigrants and immigration, we are always talking about people who matter deeply to God. We are talking about people made in the image of God—people like Hagar and my abuelita. It's easy in our current climate to allow immigrants to become nameless, faceless statistics lost in political and economic rhetoric.

A biblical response to immigrants demands that we recognize their humanity. When I began to work at World Relief, I met immigrants every day in the office. I learned their names, their telephone voices, and their faces. Day after day I heard their stories and wrote them down for petitions. I made copies of their marriage licenses, translated their birth certificates, and prepared their immigration applications. Those experiences refuted everything that textbook said about current immigration trends and most of what I'd heard in the media and church social circles. These relationships were, in part, what changed me.

Knowing names and stories activates our compassion. Without these relationships, I would continue to think of undocumented immigrants as outsiders, as the "other." In so doing, I would lose the humanity in myself as I failed to see it in them. I need these stories and relationships, not only for the sake of my immigrant community, but also for myself—in order to be changed, to see the image of God in them and in myself.

But it wasn't just these stories that changed me. Relationships are a start but not the stopping point. As a Christian, I was also radically transformed as I began to read the Bible from the margins—from the perspectives of outsiders, foreigners, and castoffs, people like Hagar. I had never realized how much the Scriptures tell the stories of people who began as strangers and then became part of the family of God. Welcome and belonging are overarching narratives of the Bible.

I have heard countless sermons about Abraham and Sarah's faith but none about Hagar, the foreigner who named God and received messengers from God. Reading the Bible through the lens of the outsider taught me truths that I lost when I relied on the readings of the dominant culture. Reading the Bible in this new way, I began to see clearly that God sees, loves, and embraces the Hagars of the world and commands us to do the same.

How might Hagar's life had been transformed by her encounter with God? I imagine she returned to Sarah's household with the knowledge that she was not only seen by God but loved by God. She knew now that her humble life mattered to the God of the universe. Living and working under Sarah's thumb must have been painful, but Sarah's disrespect and mistreatment no longer defined her. Hagar had been promised not just survival but a future among her own people, one where she would be fruitful and her young son would prosper. Like my abuelita, she went about her domestic tasks with her head held high, knowing deep in her soul that she bore God's image in the world.

6

Confirmation

Therefore, brothers and sisters, be eager to confirm your call and election. Do this and you will never ever be lost.
—2 PETER 1:10

Toward the end of Ronald Reagan's first year in office, my mother announced that we were going to the United States to join our father. We had previously visited the United States and had multiple entry tourist visas, so we flew in, arriving in Rhode Island the day before Thanksgiving in 1981 like any other tourist.

We were overjoyed to be reunited with our father, but the joy was short-lived. Providence was a small city, and there were some reports of immigration raids in areas where Latinxs worked and lived. My undocumented parents were afraid, especially since the reports seemed to become more frequent. The decision was made that after the new year, the five of us would travel across the country by bus to move to Los Angeles. There we'd live with my mother's family, my abuelita Amada and my uncle Chachi, who was my mother's youngest brother. Los Angeles was a big city where it would be easier for us to go unnoticed.

Great-Uncle Juan's funeral

Soon after we arrived in Los Angeles, I attended my first funeral. It was for my great-uncle Juan, who had died of a heart attack. I only met him once before he died, but I had heard about him often, because my mother lived in eternal gratitude to him.

Decades earlier, Great-Uncle Juan had migrated to Los Angeles, a difficult feat for an Afro-Guatemalan before the civil rights movement. Family legend has it that he crossed the border between Mexico and California in a car, sitting in the passenger seat like any other black American. The border guards did not even question him, although they could have, because he spoke English perfectly and with a Caribbean accent—a gift from his Barbadian-descended parents.

But this ability to "pass" for an American cut both ways. Since to most people he looked no different than an African American, he endured the same marginalization that they did—on top of the marginalization of being an immigrant. Even so, he and my great-aunt Teresa stayed, worked, and faithfully sent remittances to their extended family in Guatemala, including their favorite niece, my mother. Remittances may be unfamiliar to many people in North America, but many people in Latin America and many other places around the world rely on this money sent to them by relatives working abroad. For my mother and many women, remittances were essential to survival.

When I was in first grade and couldn't remember how to spell my middle name—Jeannette—my mother showed me how to write it in slow, deliberate print. She told me again that I was named Jeannette after her cousin, Great-Uncle Juan's daughter. She was so grateful for the remittances he had sent throughout the years, and she couldn't imagine how her life would have been if he hadn't paid for her nursing education.

My mother was born on the Caribbean coast of Guatemala, a place that never fails to remind me of banana bread and rice and beans cooked with grated coconut. It's hotter and more humid than much of the rest of the country, but the thick air smells like salt water and tropical fruit. At the same time, it's also a place where poverty and discrimination abound. Children grow up there only to abandon it for life in the city. My mother grew up in Izabal, with her mother and seven siblings, sometimes living with her godparents and helping out in their bakery after school.

Like most immigrant children, I was often a translator of English and American culture for my parents. One day my mother asked me what it meant to be "dirt poor"—it was a phrase she had heard other nursing assistants use at work. I explained what it meant, and she replied nonchalantly that she had been *literally* dirt poor, growing up with lots of brothers and sisters and a single mom who had only attended school until the sixth grade. "If it wasn't for my family and their remittances . . . ," she said, trailing off.

There at our great-uncle's funeral, my siblings and I sat quietly in the living room of Great-Uncle Juan's house as many adults came and went, consoling Great-Aunt Teresa. She wailed in her grief, and my abuelita walked over and patted her on the back. When you're a kid, it's unnerving to see an adult cry. I think we were too stunned to do anything but sit there and sneak a snack once in a while.

Abuelita theology

Ever since we had arrived at her little two-bedroom apartment in South Los Angeles, my maternal abuelita had taken me to church with her. I scarcely knew her, but she knew me. I was glad to attend her church just to spend time with her. Because she spoke fluent English just like her brother had, she had the freedom to attend an English-speaking church, and she did. She found a home at Crenshaw Christian Center, an African American Pentecostal church not too far from where we lived.

I did not speak any English at all, except for a few phrases like "Good morning" and "Ice cream, please." (The important ones!) But I went anyway. Later, I would reflect on what a refuge this community must have been for my abuelita. As an Afro-Guatemalan, she had often experienced rejection from white, Mestizo, and indigenous Latinx people. But here in the United States she could align herself with American blackness and find acceptance unlike any she'd ever experienced. And she found a refuge not only from discrimination but also from the hard labor she performed five days a week as a live-in housekeeper. My abuelita found rest at her home church, where she felt like everyone else and could express herself freely. There she became my spiritual mother, introducing me to a Christian tradition unlike any I had ever seen.

Latinx theologians have coined the term *abuelita theology* to refer to the work of thinking about God that is done by mothers and grandmothers. Instead of relying on formal religious instruction, to which we may not have access, many Latinx people rely on our abuelitas, those most faithful of theologians, to teach us about God.[1] Our mothers and grandmothers are the carriers of faith traditions and practices, and as in many cultures around the world, they are our first religious teachers. Sometimes abuelita theology is referred to as kitchen theology, because so much of the passing on of faith happens informally with older women, over the preparation of a meal or while performing household chores. It was abuelita theology at work when my mother and aunts would dress me in indigenous Guatemalan clothing to commemorate the feast day of the brown-skinned Virgin of Guadalupe every December 12. And it was abuelita theology that first brought me to a Pentecostal church in Los Angeles to learn about the healing power of the Holy Spirit. It was my abuelita who taught me the most about God and the value of preserving and passing on Christian traditions.

I want to see

One day, Miss Vivian, the Sunday school teacher at my grandmother's church, asked if I wanted to be baptized. I was a ten-year-old fifth grader, and Miss Vivian thought that was old enough for me to make a decision about my own life of faith. I said an enthusiastic yes. I didn't mention to her that I had already been baptized in the Catholic church in Guatemala. Miss Vivian led me through a prayer whose words I mostly didn't understand and then gave me a certificate. It looked a bit like the one I'd gotten at school for perfect attendance, and it said I was now a Christian. My abuelita was ecstatic, and so was Miss Vivian.

On the day of this second baptism—this receiving and confirming of my Christian faith—I wore a white gown. Miss Vivian asked me if I would pray with her before I went up to the baptismal pool with Pastor Price. I agreed, and she surprised me by asking *me* to pray. I shook my head, but she insisted.

"Can I pray in Spanish?" I mumbled.

She knelt down to my level and said, "Yes, but no reciting. It has to be your own prayer from your heart." Miss Vivian was always gentle but firm.

"I can say Psalm 23 in Spanish," I offered, looking at my feet.

"Can you just say some simple words to Jesus about what you want from him? Remember the story of Bartimaeus and how Jesus asked him what he wanted? All Bartimaeus said was that he wanted to see. That was his whole prayer: 'I want to see!' Just tell Jesus what you want from him."

I didn't really remember about Bartimaeus. Miss Vivian was generous, and she grossly overestimated my understanding of our Sunday school classes in English. Yet she understood that it was important for me to name my desire in Christ's presence—that this would be an important element in my spiritual life. I closed my eyes and said my first prayer in English, using my own words. "Jesus, I want to know you. Amen."

And it was true. I *did* want to know Jesus, even though I didn't quite know what that meant. Then I went forward for the full-immersion baptism, so different from the sprinkling water I'd seen poured on my brother and sister when they were babies. Pastor Price and I walked into the pool at the front of the sanctuary. He put one hand on my back and one on my head, and he dunked me backward until the water rushed over my face. "I baptize you in the name of the Father, and of the Son, and of the Holy Spirit," he said.

Then he swooped my head out of the water in one swift motion. "Welcome to your new life in Christ, little girl!" he said with a grin and ushered me out of the pool. My joyful abuelita received me on the other side, hugging me close despite my soaking wet gown.

The lonely immigrant life

Even after that, my favorite part of attending church with Abuelita remained the chocolate chip pancakes she treated me to before the service. With my limited English, I couldn't really understand everything that happened at church. But I knew it made her happy that I went with her, and I did want to know God in some way. This was our special time—our shared experience and no one else's.

My parents continued to be skeptical of Christian faith, especially the variety of faith demonstrated at this strange Pentecostal church with services that went on for hours. They worked all the time, and they were tired with that exhaustion that only immigrants who know no Sabbath can experience. This fact translated to their lack of availability to us as children, which meant that they largely ignored my church attendance. Even when they were present, they were not really there. Their adjustment to life in a new country wasn't as smooth as mine appeared to be.

My mother talked all the time about working just a little bit longer and then going back to Guatemala. She was miserable and lonely, and she missed the lively community of staff at the rehabilitation hospital where she had worked for her entire nursing career. Now she did elder care in a private home, traveling over an hour by bus each way to Studio City to spend her long days in the company of an old man who didn't speak Spanish and was slowly descending into dementia.

My father, a bright, college-educated man nicknamed "Socrates" in his university days, could only get work doing maintenance at a hotel near Disneyland. His first task of the day was to pick up garbage with a stick on the hotel grounds. For the first time in his adult life, my father didn't have a car, nor a job that required any intellectual engagement. The hotel where he worked was located in the next county, so he took a bus for the long journey back and forth.

When I was in college, studying English literature, I came across a poem called "Elegy Written in a Country Churchyard" by Thomas Gray. The speaker of the poem laments the lost potential of the poor villagers buried in a churchyard and wonders aloud what these humble people might have accomplished if they hadn't been constrained by their condition. I immediately thought of my father's lost intellectual potential as he went about his early days in America. Did the tourists staying at the hotel even suspect that they were walking past a man who read

Marx, Plato, and Dostoyevsky? Did they acknowledge him at all? My father, like all the workers upon whose labor their vacations were built, was likely invisible to them.

Since my parents' time was no longer their own and was largely devoted to work, my brother, sister, and I spent lots of time in front of the television, and no one really took notice. I have few memories of watching television in Guatemala, but in Los Angeles we watched lots of it: every cartoon from *Scooby-Doo* to *He-Man* and every TV show from *Happy Days* to *CHiPs* to *Silver Spoons*. We were rapidly learning English and loved these shows! We marveled at the egalitarian relationship between TV parents and TV kids. Were American families really like that in real life? Did American kids get to have opinions that influenced parents' decisions—about moving across the country or buying a new house or getting a dog—the way the ones on television did? We may as well have been watching aliens from another planet, so far was their experience removed from us.

Not only did they not look or sound like us or our parents; they didn't live like us. On television, American kids cared about having their own rooms and their own private space, but in our culture, your room was mostly just for sleeping. *La familia*, not the individual, is the central and most important institution in our culture.[2] Life is lived in the living room and kitchen where the family gathers. And in our cramped apartment, there were only two bedrooms but seven of us, so we had beds in the living room too.

My fourth-grade teacher once distributed a handout and asked us to draw a picture of our room on it. I slept in the living room, where my brother and sister also had bunk beds, but I didn't want her to know that. So I drew a picture of my abuelita's room, passing it off as my own and hoping the teacher wouldn't find out the truth. I felt ashamed at how different I was from the norm, and I wanted to hide my otherness from everyone at school.

It was strange for me in those early years in Los Angeles to think about my Guatemalan childhood, which had been filled with carefree time playing and exploring with neighborhood kids after school. My childhood in Los Angeles had few toys—we had left those behind in Guatemala. And playing outside, in a neighborhood where drug deals could be seen through the window of our second-story apartment, was out of the question. Besides, I couldn't have told you where my classmates lived even if you had offered me all the jelly beans in the world. The only respite from my monotonous school days and hours of watching television were those long Sundays at church.

Confirmation revisited

In the Catholic Church, three sacraments constitute initiation into the faith: baptism, communion, and confirmation. I had completed the first two sacraments within the church, but I never went through the sacrament of confirmation. According to Catholic tradition, confirmation is a special outpouring of the Holy Spirit, and the confirmed feel its effects. After confirmation, they are rooted in their identity as children of God, united with Christ and pledged to the church. There's something beautiful and reassuring about the formal process of confirmation, and I'm glad that many liturgical and mainline churches guide their members through this sacrament.

When I reflect on the process that led me to faith in Christ, I always think back to Miss Vivian and my second baptism as the moment of my own confirmation. I didn't fully understand what it meant to follow Christ, but I had moments of clarity and understanding. Like Bartimaeus, who pleaded by the side of the road asking Jesus for sight, I knew what I wanted from Jesus. Author Ruth Haley Barton has noted that Bartimaeus thinks that all he needs is sight, but Jesus recognizes that Bartimaeus needs to be restored back to his community. The blindness has kept him isolated and marginalized.[3] Sight brings him into community and into a sense of belonging that he has longed for. Jesus provides not just a physical healing but a social healing as well—one that Bartimaeus did not even know he wanted.

Like Bartimaeus, I didn't know that I had a deeper soul need to belong, and to have meaning and purpose. My days were long and dull, and I felt so much the outsider everywhere I went. But that event, in which I was plunged into the waters of my second baptism, made me feel seen by God. God saw our little apartment and the urban school where we struggled to learn English. God saw the loneliness and struggles of my parents. God saw my uncle Chachi, working at Burger King and attending classes in the evening. God saw my abuelita reading her Bible in a bedroom of a Brentwood mansion after a long day of work. And God saw me too—God saw a bewildered girl in a new country, walking to school with her brother. All I knew that day of my second baptism was that I wanted more of God than I had in that moment—and that I had the capacity to reach for more of God.

7

Joseph

The Foreigner Who Blessed Egypt

Then the Lord said to Abram, "Have no doubt that your descendants will live as immigrants in a land that isn't their own, where they will be oppressed slaves for four hundred years."
—GENESIS 15:13

I first heard about Joseph, the son of Jacob, from Andrew Lloyd Webber's musical *Joseph and the Amazing Technicolor Dreamcoat*. The musical interpretation was funny, lively, and brimming with catchy songs. I found that interpretation so compelling that it drove me to its original source, the Hebrew Scriptures. I wanted to get some answers from the Bible itself:

What was true about Joseph's story? And what had been dramatized for the amusement of musical theater fans?

Much like Ruth's story has been turned into a fairy tale, Joseph's story has been romanticized and turned into a story about a boastful little brother who needs to learn a lesson so he can become a great leader. That's what I learned from the musical. But as it turns out, Joseph's own story isn't nearly as fun or comical as the musical would have you believe. Although the musical affirms the hardships in Joseph's life in Egypt, they are mostly played for comedy, and the viewer doesn't get a sense of the injustices and the suffering he experienced as a stranger in a foreign land.

In Genesis 37, we are first introduced to Joseph. The chapter begins when he is the favored son, and it ends as he is sold into slavery by his own brothers. The rest of Joseph's story takes place in Egypt, where he suffers a series of misfortunes as a vulnerable foreigner. Joseph's story is powerful and effective because it raises questions about the goodness of God in the midst of suffering. It also depicts the human tendency to alternate between loving and fearing strangers. In his story we see the Egyptian society's movement from fear to love and then back to fear again. It is a surely a movement familiar to many North Americans who fondly remember their family's immigrant past while fearing the present wave of immigrants from different lands.

Thirteen years of suffering

First, Joseph is sold to Potiphar, Pharaoh's chief officer and commander of the royal guard. The Scriptures note that despite Joseph's unjust treatment, God always sees him and never forgets him: "The Lord was with Joseph, and he became a successful man and served in his Egyptian master's household" (Genesis 39:2). Potiphar sees that God is with Joseph and blesses his work, so Joseph rises quickly in the household. He becomes head of the household, entrusted with supervising all of it.

But Joseph is attractive, which becomes as much a liability for him as it was for his great-grandmother Sarah. Potiphar's wife becomes attracted to him and makes clear her intention to seduce him, becoming increasingly aggressive with her advances. His refusal makes her angry enough that she accuses *him* of attempting to sexually assault her. It's noteworthy that when she brings these false charges against him before her household and her husband, she highlights the fact that he is a foreigner: "The *Hebrew* slave whom you brought to us, to ridicule me, came to me; but when I raised my voice and screamed, he left his garment with me and ran outside" (Genesis 39:17-18, italics mine).

Those of us who work with immigrants are familiar with accusations like those made by Potiphar's wife. Even though the attempted sexual assault that Joseph is accused of has nothing to do with his nationality or his status as a foreigner, those facts quickly become politicized for the sake of anti-foreigner sentiments.

As I write these words, it was revealed that the alleged murderer of a young woman in the state of Iowa was an unauthorized immigrant who had harassed and stalked her as she jogged around town.[1] Rather than provoking a conversation about violence against women and the toxic masculinity that leads men to believe they're entitled to women's bodies, the current U.S. presidential administration focused on the man's immigration status, as if it were somehow the cause of this terrible crime.

Without recourse, as an enslaved person in a foreign land, Joseph does not receive due process. Instead, he is thrown into jail for a crime he didn't commit. The unknown narrator of Genesis states that God always sees Joseph and remains with him. Twice within the span of three verses we are told that "the Lord was with" Joseph, blessing his work and giving him favor with those in authority over him (Genesis 39:21-23). Joseph ends up supervising the entire prisoner population. Nonetheless, he spends years unjustly imprisoned, largely forgotten by his foreign captors.

As we reflect on this story, we may think there is a discrepancy between the narrator's continued assertions that the Lord is with Joseph and Joseph's lived reality for much of his first thirteen years in Egypt.[2] How can we be confident that God is present with such a vulnerable person when his situation doesn't change? Wouldn't God grant liberation and justice for vulnerable Joseph rather than allow him to waste away in prison?

Yet for Joseph, and for other vulnerable people throughout the world, that question may be less complicated than it seems for more privileged people who associate health and wealth with God's love and blessing. For many immigrants and others on the underside of history, God's presence in suffering isn't about complex theological arguments about theodicy or sovereignty or how bad things can happen to good people. For them, God's presence in suffering is what enables them to live. Indeed, for many who suffer, Christ on the cross offers the comfort of knowing that they serve a God who himself has known great sorrow and suffering.

The vulnerability of the immigrant

It's sad to note Joseph's many vulnerabilities as a foreigner in Egypt.

He is trafficked as a slave.

He is abused by Potiphar's wife and accused of a crime he didn't commit.

He is thrown into prison and forgotten by everyone but his God.

I'm intimately acquainted with how vulnerable immigrants are today, just as Joseph was in his time. Our very status as foreigners, authorized or not, makes us vulnerable to abuse, exploitation, and becoming victims of crimes.

Every single adult in my family was the victim of a crime within the first two years they lived in the United States. On a major street in South Los Angeles, my mother was mugged and pistol-whipped as she walked home from the bus stop after work. People passing by called an ambulance, and she was taken to a local hospital and treated for her wounds. They never caught the men who attacked her, but fortunately she didn't have critical wounds. She refused to talk to the police, using her limited English skills as an excuse.

It's not uncommon for undocumented immigrants to fear the police, believing them to be working with immigration officials in an effort to deport immigrants, or fearing that police officers are as corrupt in the United States and Canada as they are in their home countries. My mother was no different, so she opted to go home and not report the crime.

A few weeks later, my parents received a $700 bill from the hospital; it was a sobering way to learn about the steep cost of healthcare for the uninsured in the United States. My parents had no idea that six stitches could be so costly! The bill may as well have been for $700,000, since my parents didn't have the money to cover that cost and had to work out a payment plan with the hospital. This is what it means to be vulnerable: First you're attacked, and you believe that you have no legal recourse without making yourself a target of immigration officials. Then you miss vital days of work, possibly jeopardizing your job. Then you receive a medical bill so high that you're no longer barely getting by. Now you're in the red, struggling to survive.

Not long after that incident, my parents loaded up all our dirty laundry into the utility carts we used to bring our groceries home. That day they walked the half a mile to the laundromat, as they did every two weeks. My abuelita was home for the weekend from her weeklong job as a live-in housekeeper, so she stayed with my siblings and me. My little sister Michelle, who was three years old at the time, was napping, so it was the perfect opportunity for my parents to be away for a couple of hours.

Unfortunately, Michelle woke up soon after they left and was so upset to find them gone that she cried for an hour straight. My frustrated abuelita, who couldn't console her, decided we should join our parents at the laundromat. It was early evening as we headed out.

The four of us held hands, and my abuelita carried her big purse and sometimes Michelle. Our street was lively with people. I remember passing some young men bent over the open hood of a car, listening to loud music as they worked, as well as my abuelita announcing that there would be many deaf people in the future as a direct result of blaring music and big radios. We walked by a couple whispering across a chest-high fence; the young woman wore her hair in pretty braids with beads and ignored the mom calling her from the house to come inside. Finally, we could see Vermont Avenue and the big intersection up ahead. Just a few more blocks and we'd be with our parents.

As we walked past a big street light and into a dark part of the street, three young men suddenly confronted us. One of them stepped up, revealing a switchblade, and threatened my abuelita: "Give me your purse or I'll cut you up!"

I didn't have any time to react with fear or any other emotion. All I remember is my abuelita yelling "No!" into the darkening sky and running. We were all still holding hands, so my siblings and I trailed behind her, like little tin cans attached to the bumper of a car.

My abuelita didn't normally run—she considered it undignified for a person her age, even if it was for exercise. But we ran all the way to Vermont Avenue, straight into a drugstore, with her in the lead. There she related the events of the last few minutes to a cashier, exclaiming all the while that she worked hard and was not going to give her money to a hooligan. The bewildered cashier asked my abuelita if we should call the police, but she declined. She was undocumented, and didn't want to call attention to herself in any way. Instead she decided to wait for my parents in the drugstore, looking out for them from the safety of the window inside the store.

Over the next year and a half, my uncle Chachi was the victim of a mugging outside our house as he returned from work late one evening. He was badly beaten by the thieves. Similarly, my dad was attacked while he stood outside our apartment building in the late afternoon, talking with a friend. They managed to get away unscathed but were frightened nonetheless.

Research supports my family's experience: immigrants often fail to report crimes out of fear of deportation and fear of the police, and because of language barriers. A 2011 study revealed that "socially disadvantaged neighborhoods" like the one we lived in make immigrant groups more likely to become victims of crime because there are fewer social support networks. It's possible that immigrants become the targets of crime because those living around them are aware that they may be undocumented—which means they have likely come here to work, probably carry cash and won't call the police. The most common crimes committed against Latinx immigrants are wage theft (41 percent), worksite abuse by employers (22 percent), robbery (10 percent), and assault (9 percent).[3]

The U.S. government is well aware that immigrants fail to report crimes out of fear. It's for this very reason that the U visa was created in October 2000—to encourage immigrants who are victims of crime to report them to the police.[4] The visa is granted to those who report crimes that fit a certain criteria and then cooperate with the authorities who investigate and prosecute crimes. The U visa affords immigrants the benefit of a visa and a work permit, along with a pathway to citizenship. Its institution has been so successful that there's a long wait for those who qualify for one.

No such options were available to my family members. My parents, my abuelita, and my uncle continued working quietly under the radar, seeking a better life. As I reflect on these experiences, I know that God was present with us through these frightening incidents, because God is always present with those who suffer. I remember my abuelita praying Psalm 56:8: "You yourself have kept track of my misery. Put my tears into your bottle." She comforted us with a reminder that God saw our sorrow and cared deeply for us, even though our lives, much like Joseph's, seemed to be getting worse, not better. She modeled for our family the virtues evident in Joseph's life: patience when faced with unjust suffering, and perseverance when everything around you tells you to give up.

Joseph saves Egypt

Despite all his misfortunes, Joseph continues to work and bless the people around him. He even helps his fellow prisoners, although they forget him too. He had been a faithful servant to Potiphar and the prison warden, and though they recognized his gifts and his character, he remains enslaved and imprisoned. Along the way, he helps Pharaoh's baker and cupbearer, pleading with the cupbearer to petition Pharaoh on his behalf, but soon after the cupbearer's own release from prison, he forgets about Joseph too.

Joseph's situation changes only when the pharaoh begins to have disconcerting dreams. He doesn't know what to make of them and is unsettled by their content. Finally, Pharaoh's cupbearer remembers a man—a Hebrew he knew in prison who interpreted dreams. Thus Joseph is whisked away from prison to the palace, where thirteen years of slavery, abuse, and imprisonment abruptly come to an end.[5]

Joseph interprets Pharaoh's dreams, which foretell seven years of abundance and warn of seven years of famine. The pharaoh is so impressed by his wisdom and knowledge that he appoints Joseph his deputy, announcing, "Can we find a man with more God-given gifts than this one?" (Genesis 41:38). Indeed, Joseph proves himself a wise and capable leader, preparing the entire country for the coming famine.

Soon the pharaoh recognizes Joseph the Hebrew as a blessing to his country and begins to treat him as such. Pharaoh makes him the second in command in all the land, saying, "I've given you authority over the entire land of Egypt . . . no one will do anything or go anywhere in all the land of Egypt without your permission" (Genesis 41:41, 44). When famine strikes, Joseph's extended family seeks the resources that Egypt has to offer thanks to Joseph's stewardship. The foreigner who arrived as a slave and was cursed as "that Hebrew" by Potiphar's wife becomes the instrument of salvation for all of Egypt and the surrounding lands.

Later in Exodus, we learn that this welcoming posture only lasted for the lifetime of Joseph and his generation.

> Now a new king came to power in Egypt who didn't know Joseph. He said to his people, "The Israelite people are now

> larger in number and stronger than we are. Come on, let's be smart and deal with them. Otherwise, they will only grow in number. And if war breaks out, they will join our enemies, fight against us, and then escape from the land. . . . The Egyptians started to look at the Israelites with disgust and dread. So the Egyptians enslaved the Israelites. They made their lives miserable with hard labor. (Exodus 1:8-10, 12-14)

One leader sees Joseph and his Israelite family as a blessing. Later on a new leader, who doesn't know or remember what this foreigner did for Egypt, sees his descendants as a curse on the land. The unknown narrator of Exodus notes that fear becomes the driving force for the Egyptians as they deal with Israelites:

"There's so many of them! They're disgusting."

"They're stronger than we are!"

"What if they join our enemies against us?"

"We need their labor! What if they escape?"

Essentially, the Egyptians transition from *philoxenia*, the Greek word for love of foreigners, to *xenophobia*, a fear and hatred of foreigners. From love to fear: this is a transition familiar to many of us. The United States, for example, formerly welcomed refugees without controversy. For many Americans, refugees were the "good immigrants" because they arrived in the United States with documented permission—the "legal" way—often fleeing persecution. But in the course of several years, as fears around terrorism and national security have been stoked by our political leaders, the refugee program in the United States has been decimated. All of this has occurred as the United States has become less and less hospitable to all immigrants, regardless of status. From *philoxenia* to *xenophobia*. From love to fear.

Fear has become the default in the current immigration conversation in North America, even for followers of Jesus, who are called to love our neighbors as ourselves. The Bible speaks to the need for *philoxenia* repeatedly, from Exodus all the way to Hebrews: "Keep loving each other like family. Don't neglect to open up your homes to guests [strangers or foreigners], because by doing this some have been hosts to angels without knowing it" (Hebrews 13:1-2).

So how do we move from *xenophobia* back to *philoxenia*? Professor Richard Beck says, "We don't show hospitality to *be like* Jesus. We show hospitality to *welcome* Jesus."[6] Many of us are familiar with spiritual disciplines that bring us closer to God—disciplines like prayer, study, and meditation are critical to our growth. But while these move us closer to God, they often fail to move us closer to one another. For that we need a spiritual discipline of hospitality, one that will help us draw near to those we fear, those who make us uncomfortable, and those we've even learned to hate. Beck says that such a spiritual practice will expand "the bandwidth of our kindness and compassion. Our emotions change when we begin to adopt practices that slowly, over time, reconfigure our feelings and affections."[7]

When we open ourselves up to friendships with immigrants and take intentional steps to know and be known in mutuality, we widen the circle of our affections. Suddenly, immigrants are no longer a burden or a drain on our economy, but a Ruth, a Hagar, or a Joseph to be loved. They become multidimensional people to us—friends who enrich our lives with their very selves. We welcome them and simultaneously welcome Christ and his joy.

Indeed, when the Egyptians welcomed the Israelites, they welcomed God and God's blessing into their midst. And when they rejected the Israelites and oppressed them, they rejected God's very self, even without realizing it. Jesus often comes to us in disguise, as he himself says in Matthew 25: he is sometimes a prisoner, a sick person, a naked person, a hungry person, a thirsty person, or an immigrant (verses 35-36).

If we learn anything from Joseph and his suffering, it is to welcome and embrace Jesus in disguise. Vulnerable people may present themselves before us in great need and in a strange façade that we fear: a hijab, a sari, or a sombrero. But John's first letter tells us that we can't love God, whom we do not see, if we don't love one another. There is no fear in love; perfect love casts out fear (1 John 4:18-20). Welcoming and embracing our immigrant neighbors is how we will transition back to *philoxenia*.

8

Anointing the Sick

If any of you are sick, they should call for the elders of the church, and the elders should pray over them, anointing them with oil in the name of the Lord.

—**JAMES 5:14**

Many of the healing shrines around the world are devoted to Mary, the mother of Jesus. One of the most famous Catholic shrines is Our Lady of Lourdes in France. Sick pilgrims claim to have experienced miraculous recoveries in the healing waters of Lourdes since the nineteenth century, when Mary is said to have appeared there to a young peasant girl named Bernadette.

In Guatemala, Catholics often petition Mary as Santa María, Madre de Dios, to intercede for them when they need a healing miracle. For many Catholics, Mary seems to embody the feminine heart of God, who cares tenderly for the sick and has a mother's compassion for those who suffer.

When I started spending time in evangelical Christian circles, I often wondered why they did not honor Mary. I knew that some evangelicals thought that Catholics worship Mary and were thus suspicious of Catholics. But I began to wonder: Shouldn't the mother of God, the one who bore Christ, hold a special place for *all* Christians? Isn't Mary, who responded so willingly to God's call, an important person in the story of the church? Doesn't she reveal to us something about the gentle, nurturing side of God?

It made sense to me that people would petition Mary to pray for them when they were desperate for someone they love to be healed and when they had exhausted all other possibilities. It made sense to me because Santa María is whom I turned to when my own mother faced cancer and when none of the treatments seemed to be working.

The Sunshine State

I divide time into two parts: before my mother died and after my mother died. Her death was such a defining moment in my life that even today, decades later, I have dreams that she is still alive and involved in my everyday life. I wake up wrapped in grief that she's actually gone. These are the only dreams I have in Spanish.

At first, I didn't take her illness very seriously. Her own mother, my abuelita Amada, had also had breast cancer, and she recovered and went on to live another twenty-five years. Besides, my mother was young, only thirty-seven years old.

Youth is supposed to make you more resilient in the face of illness. The morning she had her first surgery, a mastectomy, she dropped us off at our suburban Florida high school as she did every other day. I intentionally avoided discussing the cancer and the surgery, because I wanted to pretend it wasn't real. That day at school, I battled faint regret at not having kissed her or wished her well, but my teenage optimism told me everything would be fine.

We had moved to Florida in the mid-1980s. Los Angeles had been a difficult place for my parents, with long commutes and difficult adjustments. For a time it was a good place to wait for the immigrant visas my uncle Hugo, my father's brother, had filed for us. My uncle was married to a U.S. citizen, my aunt Judy, and through the process of family-based immigration he had sponsored his own parents and all his siblings. We waited two and a half years for our visas, and when our number came up, we flew to Guatemala for our interview at the American embassy in Guatemala City. Were we to apply today, our wait would be more like thirteen years, not two. And if we were Chinese, Indian, Mexican, or Filipino immigrants, our wait would be closer to twenty-three years.

Our family became documented the way most immigrants to the United States do: through family-based immigration. It is the cornerstone of the Immigration and Nationality Act, the federal law that governs immigration. According to the National Immigration Forum, 65 percent of immigrants adjust their status as we did: through a relative's sponsorship.[1] Contrary to what is often reported in the news, there is no such thing as "chain migration," because only immediate relatives are eligible for sponsorship. My uncle sponsored my father, who then extended that sponsorship to us. But Uncle Hugo could not have sponsored his cousins, aunts and uncles, grandparents, or more distant relatives. Now that I work for an organization that serves immigrants, I realize how fortunate we were to have had a close relative who was a citizen and earned enough income to sponsor us. So many immigrants have no such ties and, therefore, no immigration solution.

Our brief time as undocumented immigrants came to a joyful end, and my parents began to think of the kinds of things people with no fears of deportation are free to think about: buying a house, finding a Little League team for my brother, and getting us music lessons. We had left South Los Angeles and had moved to a suburban neighborhood in the San Gabriel Valley. But the prices of homes in Southern California were far above what my parents could afford. They were afraid they would never be able to become homeowners there. Fortunately, our new green cards, given to all permanent residents, provided freedom to move safely about the country, and so we did. During a brief stay in Rhode Island with my father's family, my parents began to explore places to live.

A trip to Florida in the month of February settled it for them. Florida enchanted them; it was lush, tropical, affordable, and most importantly, friendly to immigrants. At that time the biggest immigrant populations in Florida were Cubans and Puerto Ricans—both Latinx groups that have always been documented individuals in the United States. Cubans were considered refugees from their communist homeland, and

Puerto Ricans are U.S. citizens from an American territory, so they are considered migrants, not immigrants. This meant that the anti-immigrant sentiment we had experienced in California was largely absent in Florida. Nobody assumed we were "illegal" or ever had been. Even the governor was named Martinez, a common surname in Spanish-speaking countries! My parents didn't hesitate with their plans to move south to the immigrant-friendly Sunshine State.

My mother was giddy with excitement about the prospect of having her own house, as she did in Guatemala. She couldn't wait to plant her own garden, as she had longed for a place where she could grow the Guatemalan cooking herbs she couldn't find at the grocery store. Growing things and running her hands through fertile soil were her passions, and the screened porch of our new house would be an ideal place for her houseplants. My father had visited our future schools in Seminole, a suburb of Tampa, and had been pleased to see new buildings at the high school and an elementary school not too far from our house. If this is what it was to live the American dream, my parents were well underway.

Latina mothers are often depicted in the media as overly affectionate women who are great dancers, have fiery tempers, and spend a busy life in the kitchen. That was not my mother. She was a slender and reserved woman who hated cooking and domestic work in general—though she made exceptions to prepare the traditional Guatemalan food that she missed. She would happily fry plantains or make salsa from scratch. But more than anything, my mother loved working as a nurse. If there's one thing that was true about her, it is how hard she worked outside our home. In her spare time, she enjoyed watching sports like tennis and baseball. My favorites memories of my mother are of her sitting at Dodger Stadium, booing the opposing team or yelling at the umpire. Part of Florida's appeal for our family was that there was serious talk that Tampa Bay would soon get its own baseball team.

Two months before we departed for Florida, my mother suspected something was wrong. She had found a lump and knew that she needed to see a doctor and get it checked out. With all the packing and transition to a new state, she decided to wait until after we were settled in our new house in our new state. What could go wrong? All her dreams were coming true. She had a little house in Guatemala, and now she had a little house in Florida. A delay of a few months couldn't be a big deal for a young woman like her.

That decision likely cost her her life. I often replay that scenario in my head and wish I could go back and force her to go to the doctor. I would remind her that we had a family history of cancer and that she shouldn't assume she'd be fine. But as a young girl I had no such presence of mind, and I agreed with my mother that she could wait to get the lump checked until after we were in our new home.

Those first years in Florida with my family are marked by heartache and grief. Florida was supposed to be the place where my parents' dreams came true; instead, it became the location of their undoing. I don't even like to visit Florida anymore—it's as if the whole state is tainted by tragedy. Life in California had been hard for my parents, but I'd had a pretty good life. I liked my school and my friends. I had my abuelita and the assurance her strong faith provided, along with my own growing faith. When we left, I lost all those valuable connections, and once again I felt untethered and lost to God.

Less than six months

My mother did not have a prolonged illness. She went through multiple surgeries and died two years after she was diagnosed. The cancer was unstoppable. It was like a tsunami: one moment you're safe on dry land and the next you're drowning. The cancer was drowning her; we watched her become frail and emaciated. She stopped working, then driving, then eating; she didn't even have the energy to watch baseball on television, which used to be her favorite thing to do.

My abuelita, who was now staying with us to see my mother through her illness, kept assuring us that she would get better through the efforts of prayer and modern medicine. But Abuelita also had natural remedies in mind; she had cancer-curing herbs sent to her from an indigenous healer in Guatemala and made foul-smelling teas from them. My mother drank them eagerly, hoping for the cure they promised.

By the summer of my seventeenth birthday I was driving my mother to her chemotherapy appointments, trusting what my abuelita said. But I could not believe that my eyes deceived me; I couldn't shake the uncertainty I felt about my abuelita's confidence in my mother's complete healing.

My doubts finally led me to ask my mother's oncologist myself, while I waited one day during one of her chemotherapy treatments. I caught him as he walked by the nursing station.

"Dr. Williams, do you have a minute?" I asked. "I'd like to ask you about my mother, Myra González."

"Sure," he replied, not looking up from the papers in his hands, "but only a minute."

"When is she going to start getting better and looking like herself again? We're really worried about her."

He looked up at me incredulously. He put the papers he was holding on the desk counter and then looked back at me intently. "She's not going to get better," he said. "The chemotherapy is our last effort, and it's not working so far. Your mother has less than six months to live."

I remember that moment with the precision and clarity I've heard people say they remember the birth of their child. I remember the color of the chairs in the waiting room; the dirt smudges on the white desk at the nurses' station; the smell of rubbing alcohol wafting into the room. I remember the careful way Dr. Williams laid down his papers, and the weighty look on his face when he looked up at me. I don't think he knew I was not yet even seventeen.

On the way home from the hospital, I was unusually quiet. From the corner of my eye I could see my mother occasionally wincing in pain and resting her head on the passenger side window. When we got home she went to her bedroom to rest, and I marched straight to the kitchen to talk to my father and abuelita. I yelled out at them everything the doctor had told me. I couldn't believe they had kept this news from my siblings and me, and worst of all, from my mother!

They stood by their decision. Having grown up primarily in the United States, I didn't know that it's a common belief in

Guatemala that telling a person of their diagnosis and prognosis will affect the person's will to live and minimize their fight for life.

Abuelita told me in no uncertain terms that I was forbidden from mentioning anything from my conversation with the doctor to my mother or my siblings. "Dios es amor. He will heal her," she proclaimed. "We just have to have faith."

Keeping the faith

By then I had lost my budding faith and any trace of optimism. How could a good God let my mother suffer like this? I found that I couldn't be in a house of what felt like pretense and lies, so I spent most of my time out of the house in any activity I could join. As the summer wore on, more and more relatives came from all over the country to be with my mother. Even my aunt Gladys came from Mexico City. Abuelita felt it was important for us to be in church praying for my mother, and she had found an evangelical, Pentecostal church in our neighborhood when she had visited the previous year. I often went with her because she never learned to drive, and I soon made friends with the youth pastor and other kids my age.

The people in that church community were mostly white. They were extremely kind and supportive, even if they often did not understand our cultural traditions. The interim pastor, Andy, often came over to our house to pray for my mother. By this time, she was receiving end-of-life care. The hospital bed didn't fit in my parents' bedroom, so it was placed in the living room. There was an oxygen machine next to it to aid in her breathing since the cancer had spread to her lungs, and she was given morphine every few hours to treat her pain. My abuelita would sit at her bedside and read Psalm 91 aloud in Spanish:

> El que habita al abrigo del Altísimo
> Morará bajo la sombra del Omnipotente.
> Diré yo a Jehová: Esperanza mía, y castillo mío;
> Mi Dios, en quien confiaré.
> Él te librará del lazo del cazador,
> De la peste destructora.
> Con sus plumas te cubrirá,
> Y debajo de sus alas estarás seguro;
> Escudo y adarga es su verdad.
> No temerás el terror nocturno,
> Ni saeta que vuele de día.
> (Psalm 91:1-5 RV1960)

In her lucid moments, my mother would look at Abuelita as she read, but mostly she slept. I found solace in my abuelita's reading. I can still hear her voice in my head, reading quietly as the oxygen machine hummed in the background.

When I prayed, I did so alone, in my room, with a rosary I had bought on our last visit to Guatemala. I prayed with desperation and yearning, petitioning Santa María to intercede for my mother. Even as I attended an evangelical youth group, it seemed natural to default to the Catholicism of my earliest Christian experiences. There in my bedroom, I would think about the pilgrims who journey each January to the Basilica de Esquipulas in eastern Guatemala. There, beneath a wooden image of Christ on the cross that has been blackened by soot from candles over the years, these seekers light candles. They pray for their departed loved ones and petition for those who are sick or suffering. I asked my mother's good friend, Pia, who was visiting us from Guatemala, to go to Esquipulas for me when she returned home. It gave me comfort to know she would do so. Perhaps the Black Christ of Esquipulas would come through with a miracle.

Trusting in God

In the Catholic Church, when people are sick, their priests anoint them with oil. Clergy in other traditions do this as well, even if anointing with oil is not always viewed as a sacrament. Anointing is usually the last sacrament that people receive in their lives. According to the catechism, the anointing provides courage, strength, and peace in the face of illness and helps the sick person to trust in God no matter what happens. It's a rite performed to convey God's grace to the recipient through the power of the Holy Spirit, and its roots go all the way back to Mark 6:13, in which Jesus sends out the disciples two by two to extend his mission: "They cast out many demons, and they anointed many sick people with olive oil and healed them."

Because many Latinx cultures are so closely tied to the Catholic Church, we have grown used to tangible signs, like candles and rosaries and crucifixes, even if we have joined other Christian traditions. To Latinx believers within the evangelical church, worship can sometimes feel disconnected from spiritual realities, as if we must imagine everything. In the Catholic Church, the smoke from the burning incense represents the prayers of the people rising up to heaven, reflecting Psalm 141:2: "Let my prayer stand before you like incense." But in the Protestant church, we just have to know our prayers rise; there's no symbol that represents that reality.

I don't know if Pastor Andy knew that our family needed a discernible sign, but one day he came to our house, along with a group of people from the church, to pray for my mother. There in the living room, Pastor Andy anointed my mother with oil, and the group prayed for her healing. My abuelita and other relatives joined them. I have no way of knowing what this meant to my mother, but it was perhaps the only time I ever heard her speak about her faith. Maybe she was inspired by a tangible sign of grace. I don't know exactly what she said, because by this time her voice had grown soft and raspy, and I was standing far from her.

Years later, after I began following Jesus with more intention, this memory provided me with so much consolation. The knowledge that my mother had made steps toward Christ meant she was now at peace, with no more pain, and dwelling in Christ's loving arms.

But this reassurance didn't take away the many questions I had about the goodness of God in a world where the mother I needed so much died so young. Just as Joseph in Egypt knew that God was with him, I now have a profound sense that Jesus, the Man of Sorrows, was with me through the difficult years shortly before and after she died, and saw me in my grief. He was present to me even though I wasn't present to him. Still, this singular event became my greatest barrier to faith as a teenager and young adult. I felt like the desperate father who came to Jesus, pleading, "I believe; help my unbelief!" (Mark 9:24 NRSV).

And eventually Jesus answered.

9

The Syrophoenician Woman

The Foreigner with Sass

The Lord says:
Act justly and do what is righteous,
because my salvation is coming soon,
and my righteousness will be revealed.
—ISAIAH 56:1

When I first began reading the Bible, there was a lot I didn't understand. Leviticus and Numbers seemed incredibly confusing, with their detailed and esoteric information about things like the number of people in a clan or the cleansing rituals for those afflicted with leprosy. Thankfully, I could always count on the Gospels to be clear. Jesus communicated hard truths, but he didn't confuse me the way other parts of the Bible did.

The one exception to that rule? The story of the Syrophoenician woman in Mark 7:24-30. This conversation between a woman and Jesus baffled me like no other story in the New Testament, and for a time I resented its presence there in the middle of the Gospels, which otherwise illumined my newfound faith in Jesus. But this story upended everything I thought I knew about him.

The story opens in the region around Tyre, a distinctively non-Jewish place in the north; it was a large Phoenician port city of Syria.[1] The text tells us that Jesus has gone into a house to retreat and doesn't want anyone to know it. But apparently he can't hide, because his reputation as a healer precedes him. A foreign woman—a Greek of Syrophoenician origin and, presumably, a pagan—hears about Jesus and finds him. She falls at his feet and begs him to heal her demon-possessed daughter.

Unlike Jairus, a fellow Jewish man and a leader in the synagogue, who also falls at Jesus' feet begging for his daughter's healing just two chapters earlier, this woman's request is seemingly an affront to Jesus and his honor status. Ched Myers writes that "no woman, and especially a gentile, unknown and unrelated to this Jew, would have dared invade his privacy . . . to seek a favor."[2] This fact alone makes this woman's boldness in seeking an audience and a favor from Jesus quite admirable. Unfamiliar as we are with social propriety in the ancient Near East, most of us miss the scandal in this encounter.

This Greek Syrophoenician mother suffers a layered systemic oppression. She falls under multiple marginalized social identities: ethnicity, gender, and status. The demon possession in her immediate family also makes her unclean, or contaminated, so this woman experiences xenophobia, sexism, classism, and religious discrimination. The stigma of her unique situation would not have been lost on Mark's original readers.

Now the story gets complicated and more than a little confusing. Jesus, who was interrupted often and received numerous petitions for healings and the casting out of demons, responds to the woman in a way that seems, at best, uncharitable. She is a desperate mother pleading for help, and he says, "The children have to be fed first. It isn't right to take the children's bread and toss it to the dogs" (Mark 7:27). He sees her and, in essence, calls her a "dog." Then Jesus states his own understanding of his mission: the Jewish people ("the children") have priority, and she doesn't.

Some biblical scholars assert that Jesus' rebuff of this unnamed woman is understandable, as it reflects the ethnic, cultural, and sociopolitical hostility between the Jewish people and their foreign neighbors.[3] Others point out that Jesus, while fully human and fully divine, must be having one of his human moments in this passage. These interpreters read the passage at face value: that Jesus is being dismissive of and even downright racist toward her.[4]

It's difficult to say what Jesus is thinking in this moment. Just a few verses earlier, he had stated emphatically, "Nothing outside of a person can enter and contaminate a person in God's sight; rather, the things that come out of a person contaminate the person" (Mark 7:15). Wait. Shouldn't this woman's "outside" characteristics—unclean, female, foreigner—not be counted against her?

This earlier verse, as well as what we believe about Jesus' compassion more generally, leads other commentators to interpret Jesus' harsh words toward her as theater, of sorts. Jesus responds to her as his disciples and other Jewish men in his day would have: with scorn and dismissiveness. Performing the discriminatory norms of his day allows him to then call attention to them later in the story. In other words, he reveals to his listeners the exclusionary practices of their culture by enacting them for a moment so that he can later call attention to them.

I like to think of this encounter in this way: as Jesus' teaching opportunity for the people around him in this moment. Yet at times I'm not so sure. I have to admit that I'm uncomfortable when I read this story. This is not the Jesus who called the little children to come to him or affirmed and healed a bleeding woman who touched him. I have a hard time reconciling the Jesus in this passage with the one presented in the rest of the Gospels. He's God in the flesh, who lived a life without sin. Is it possible for him to have a lapse in compassion in this narrative?

Couldn't he just tell her he came for the Jewish people? Does he have to suggest that she is a "dog," however indirectly? Even though Greeks and Romans like her didn't despise dogs the way Semitic peoples did, she must know that Jesus is leveling an insult at her that is extremely offensive within his own culture.[5] Is that how he sees her? Yes, she's a woman. Yes, she's a foreigner. Yes, she's unclean by Jewish standards. But in this moment of crisis in her life, shouldn't the fact that her child is suffering trump everything else? At least for Jesus? Thankfully, this is not the end of the story. Thankfully, Jesus is facing a bold woman who will not let herself be dismissed so easily.

Alejandra's story

I met a similarly bold and courageous woman while working at the World Relief immigration legal clinic in Baltimore. Like me, Alejandra was from Guatemala, so we had an instant bond, even though she was considerably younger than me. My job focused on speaking to churches about immigration, and I only worked in the clinic's office as needed. So my meetings with clients, although they happened regularly, were somewhat unpredictable. On the Tuesday morning that I met Alejandra, our office was packed with immigrants seeking legal assistance. I was tasked with doing "intakes": taking notes on a person's story and immigration situation in order to pass on the information to an immigration legal services representative.

Alejandra sat down in my tiny office, and I began to ask her questions about her immigration journey. When did you enter the United States? Were you admitted at a port of entry, or did you cross the border unlawfully? Do you have any immediate relatives in the United States who are U.S. citizens or permanent residents? What immigration petitions have you filed in the past?

When we got to that last question, Alejandra mentioned that she hadn't filed anything but wanted to apply for asylum. Asylum is an immigration solution given to those who can prove they have a credible fear of persecution in their own country. The caveat is that persecution which qualifies one for asylum is defined only as persecution resulting from one's race, religion, nationality, political opinion, or membership in a particular social group. Essentially, an asylee and a refugee are no different except that asylees present themselves at a U.S. border or after they have already been admitted to the United States, whereas refugees to the United States arrive in the country already with permission to migrate permanently.

From our brief conversation, I already knew that Alejandra wasn't facing persecution for any of the categories except, perhaps, membership in a particular social group. Usually, the "social group" category is reserved for people who, for example, were child soldiers, family members of political dissidents, members of ethnic groups targeted because of their faith, or women with a credible fear of genital mutilation.

Alejandra began to relate her story to me. She had lived peacefully in Guatemala City with her parents and sister with no dreams of leaving her home country. As a teen, she began to see more and more *maras*, or gangs, moving into their neighborhood. Gang activity in the Northern Triangle of Guatemala, Honduras, and El Salvador has escalated dramatically in the last decade, displacing hundreds of thousands of people and creating an insurmountable challenge for local law enforcement and the national governments. *Maras* are so much like organized crime that they are called the "mafia of the poor." According to one human rights report, the insecurity of the nations in the Northern Triangle "closely reflects patterns of control and confrontation by organized armed actors." Each local gang, the report says, "operates with a large degree of autonomy, using violence to control core territory, impose its will on local inhabitants and carry out extortion."[6]

A tragic aspect of Central America's gang problem is that it doesn't originate in Central America; it was born in the United States. The MS-13 gang, one of the most violent in the Western Hemisphere, was founded in Los Angeles in the 1980s by children of Salvadoran immigrants. These immigrant parents fled their country because of the brutal civil war—a war, much like Guatemala's, mostly funded by the United States.[7] Once in Los Angeles, the children of these immigrants became the casualties of marginalization and underfunded social programs in poor neighborhoods; they formed gangs to deal with their social exclusion and ended up in prison with hardened criminals. There they learned how to form real gangs. Eventually, they were deported back to Central America in the late 1980s and 1990s, where they re-formed their gangs and created a sophisticated criminal enterprise.[8]

These *maras* were well known to Alejandra's parents, and of course her parents sought to protect their daughters. Her father would walk them to school every morning. In the afternoon, however, when her father was at work, she and her sister would make their way home on their own. One gang member began to take a particular interest in Alejandra. He was a leader in his gang, and he began to pursue Alejandra aggressively. She refused his advances, knowing he was much older and a dangerous man, but he didn't accept her refusals. He would threaten other men who spoke to her, announcing that she was his girlfriend. Alejandra stood up for herself at first. Defiantly she would declare to him, "I'm not your girlfriend. You don't own me, so stop bothering me. Déjeme en paz! Leave me alone!"

But he was relentless; he began to follow her home or whenever she left her house. She was anxious and afraid whenever she had to go outside, so she missed days of school at a time in order to avoid him. One day, he approached her on the street when she and her sister walked home from school. His fellow gang members separated her from her sister, and he threatened Alejandra. He told her that he would kidnap and rape her younger sister if she didn't become his girlfriend. He reminded her that he had it in his power to kill her parents. Then he released her to think about her choices.

Alejandra relayed the whole story to her parents through hysterical tears. They had seen members of the *maras* make good on their threatening promises. They also knew the police would be no help. They had watched as neighbors and friends filed police reports that made it into the hands of gang members, who then severely punished and sometimes even murdered those who had filed them. There is so much corruption within police forces that it's impossible to trust them. So Alejandra decided her only recourse to protect her family was to become the gang leader's girlfriend.

Over the next few months, Alejandra was repeatedly raped by the gang member. He continued to threaten that he would harm her whole family. She grew despondent and depressed, and she stopped going to school and often battled suicidal thoughts. "I felt so dirty," Alejandra told me. "Some days I felt so dirty that I thought I would never feel clean again."

When she discovered she was pregnant, the gang member lost interest in her and moved on to someone else.

In the spring, she gave birth to a son, Diego, and continued to live with her parents, who helped her take care of him. She continued to struggle with anxiety and depression, blaming herself for the rapes. Even so, she gave everything that she had to raising her little boy. She finished high school and received training to become a bookkeeper. Her dreams of a university education had vanished when her baby was born, but she had found a decent job. Some semblance of normalcy returned to her life, though she was still aware of the extortion and violence in her neighborhood.

Everything changed one afternoon when Alejandra took her son, now a toddler, to a nearby park to play. Several gang members were gathered there; among them, the man who had raped her and threatened her family. He saw her and approached her. He pointed at Diego and yelled, "That's my son!" She was frightened and didn't respond. He continued, "That boy is coming home to live with his father." Alejandra gathered her son and ran home, while the gang members laughed at her fearful escape. Then the texts and phone calls began, threatening to take Diego from her. She changed her cell phone number, but somehow the gang members found out her new one. She could never be sure if they intended to take Diego from her or just wanted to terrify her with the threat.

When people began to follow her to work, Alejandra's parents suggested she leave Guatemala and head north to the United States with her son. They now had family friends there in the States, friends who had also fled the growing violence in their country, and she could stay with them in Maryland. They hired a human smuggler, a *coyote*, to get her to the United States.

It took Alejandra two months and $7,000, which her parents had borrowed, to make the journey with her little son. She understood full well that she'd have to pay that debt somehow, or else her parents would lose their home. Now she was safe from gang violence and living in Baltimore.

Our small office doesn't take asylum cases, because they require time and resources we simply don't have. So we referred Alejandra to a nonprofit immigration legal office that works specifically with immigrant women who have experienced sexual violence. I don't know what happened with Alejandra's case after she left our office, nor where she is living or how she is faring today. But I do know that out of all the immigration solutions available, asylum is one of the most difficult to get. As much as Alejandra had suffered, and as much as I believed her, she had no proof of what she had been through in Guatemala. There were no police reports, no letters, and no texts. The U.S. system requires proof of persecution, and it's rare that those who flee to U.S. borders have any such evidence.

I often think about Alejandra. She was so young but so strong and resilient. Even though she had trained as a bookkeeper and had only ever worked in an office setting in Guatemala, she took a job in an industrial laundry in Baltimore, washing linens for local hospitals. It was grueling work that required her to be on her feet in suffocating heat for hours on end. But she went to work every day, and she cared for her son, and she sent money to her parents. After all she had endured, she continued to persevere to create a safer life for herself and her son. I often wonder where she is now—where she is living and how she is doing. I wonder how often she stops to think about all the trauma she has suffered. I know that Jesus sees Alejandra and values her struggle. It grieves me to know how the immigration laws in the United States and Canada fail women like Alejandra.

Sass and the Syrophoenician woman

What I love about the story of the Syrophoenician woman in Mark's gospel is that Jesus does *not* fail her. Like Alejandra, this brave woman has a child to protect. So when Jesus says the children, not the dogs, must be fed first, she is undeterred and responds with a sassy comeback, "Lord, even the dogs under the table eat the children's crumbs" (Mark 7:28). She acknowledges the priority of the Jewish people in Jesus' mission, but she also makes a case for inclusion for foreigners like her.[9] This disrespectful backtalk is a surprising response given the woman's status, but it's a brilliant one. Theologian Mitzi Smith calls the Syrophoenician woman's sass "truth-telling with an attitude."[10]

Sass, frankly, is all she has. She won't be silenced, and she resists with her *logos*, or words, her marginalization as a woman, a foreigner, and an unclean person.[11] The woman's answer taps into Jesus' compassion and turns her into an advocate for her child. In some sense, her sass turns her into an advocate for all women who would be denied wholeness, justice, and respect because of laws and traditions.[12] She stands up for her people's inclusion at Jesus' table. But how will the rabbi respond to a foreign woman who has broken protocol and stepped out of her place?

Though he is a master of verbal retorts himself, and though he has bested men who were teachers of the law or civil leaders, Jesus concedes the argument. "Good answer!" one translation says he responded (Mark 7:29 CEB). Another puts it this way: "For saying that, you may go—the demon has left your daughter" (NRSV). And the woman goes. She returns home and finds her little girl lying in bed, no longer tormented by a demon and restored to wholeness.

Did the woman remind Jesus of his own earlier assertions about what contaminated a person and required exclusion from his kingdom? Did she persuade him? Or did she play a part in Jesus' theatrical, teachable moment for his followers? We don't know, and biblical interpreters have debated these questions for centuries. But no matter how you choose to interpret Jesus' initial response to the woman, what *is* clear is that he grants her request. Jesus affirms her. He says she is right. He grants her daughter health and wholeness and liberation, and he does so because of her words, not her faith. Her *logos* is what he credits for his apparent change of heart.

I imagine that woman returning to her life with an assurance that her life matters to God. She spoke to God the way she'd speak to a friend or family member, and he had received her words and invited her to the meal prepared for the children of the house. And she was exactly the kind of foreigner nobody wanted in the family: a contaminated woman with a need. Many more foreigners would be included in Jesus' mission, but she was one of the first.

Jesus' encounter with this woman is a beautiful example of God's economy. There is food for the native citizens, and there is food for the foreigners. There is plenty for you, and there is plenty for me. Jesus' actions challenge a scarcity mindset that leads people to exclude the immigrant because they fear they won't have enough. Theologian Ched Myers says, "The collective honor of Jesus' people is no longer the ultimate value; rather, fundamental *human* solidarity is more important, including embracing persons furthest from one's own group. . . . Jesus models a way that transgresses borders, embraces the 'other,' and embodies the dream of God by welcoming everyone to the table."[13] Jesus in his ministry inaugurated a new day—a new social order whose cornerstone would be inclusion for all, citizen and foreigner alike.

The Syrophoenician woman's demands for the crumbs from the table come to us today. Christians seeking to live lives faithful to the Scriptures have no choice but to welcome immigrants, trusting in the abundance of God's economy. But some people argue that this requirement to welcome immigrants is strictly for the church, not nations. While it's true that nations can make decisions that churches don't have to, it makes good economic sense for nations to have this posture as well. According to a 2018 report, amid all the hateful and unwelcoming rhetoric around immigrants in the United States, there are still more jobs than American workers to fill them: 6.7 million jobs to 6.35 million workers.[14] Nations can concede priority for citizens while also acknowledging that there is room for everyone, even the foreigner in need.

In many Western countries today, fears of scarcity around jobs, services, and resources seem to be the default response to immigration. It's understandable that people who feel economically imperiled are on the lookout for explanations for their situation. But the work of leading economists, demographers, and scholars reveals that immigrants actually create jobs.[15] The very act of leaving your country and starting over is entrepreneurial, and it's probably why immigrants are more likely than the native-born to start their own businesses.[16] Furthermore, international immigration is one of the only ways that U.S. cities in decline have been restored and repopulated.[17] Although it may seem counterintuitive to some, welcoming immigrants is good for countries and their economies. And that's because in *God's* economy, there is always enough.

Raising our voices for immigrants

When I consider the Syrophoenician woman's story and Alejandra's story side by side, I consider the fact that Alejandra spoke up and was almost crushed by her oppressor. When she arrived in the United States, she had to speak up and tell her story again. She had to talk about an incredibly traumatic and painful experience in order to fulfill a requirement of the only immigration process available to her: asylum. Neither were her efforts successful, as far as I know. The system she encountered was unjust and outdated.

In contrast, the Syrophoenician woman spoke up and found liberation and restoration. She experienced healing and comfort because the person she encountered was just and good. She and Alejandra stand in the tradition of biblical women like Vashti, Esther, and Mary, Jesus' own mother, who said an enthusiastic yes to the difficult call of God on her life.[18] These are women who spoke up and, in some case, risked everything to raise their voices on behalf of themselves and others.

But speaking up is not a magic bullet; it doesn't always ensure the outcome we desire.

Queen Vashti refused to be treated like a sexual object in front of the king and his cronies. She stood up for herself—and lost her title and probably her life (Esther 1).

Queen Esther lived in fear and risked her life, unsure of what would happen if she spoke up to defend her people from a tyrant king (Esther 2–9).

Mary said yes to becoming the bearer of God's own Son, not sure if her betrothed, Joseph, would divorce her publicly and have her stoned to death. She survived to see that son, the flesh of her flesh, tortured and murdered by the state (Luke 1, 23).

Speaking up can be painful, but it ensures our own humanity, the preservation of our souls. In his book *Between the World and Me*, Ta-Nehisi Coates drives home this point when he advises his son on the importance of resistance to oppression: "You are called to struggle not because it assures you victory but because it assures you an honorable and sane life."[19]

Those in the United States who advocate for immigrants understand that we face insurmountable odds. As I write, we face a presidential administration that is decimating the refugee resettlement program. We face border agents who refuse people like Alejandra their right to apply for asylum; a zero-tolerance policy at the border that separates immigrant children from their parents; the cancellation of Temporary Protected Status for those who have fled disasters or political instability in their countries; the criminalization of immigration; and on and on. The disappointment, the losses, and the dehumanization of immigrant lives can be soul-crushing.

But we don't give up, and we don't lose hope. We understand, just as the Syrophoenician woman did, that if unjust systems are going to be dismantled, it will require us, as biblical scholar Mitzi Smith says, "to sass and talk back, risking retaliation and even life." Smith reminds us that "unjust systems and the people who prosper from them don't just wake up one day and decide that they are tired of the benefits. . . . The silence of the oppressed (and their allies) will never topple the master's house."[20] So we talk back to our churches, our friends, and our legislators, praying for a change of heart. Perhaps we even talk back to Jesus, asking for justice for his name's sake. It was he who told us that those who hunger and thirst for righteousness will be filled.

This foreign, unclean woman was seen and heard by God. She fought for her and her people's inclusion in Jesus' mission. And she got it. If the immigrant story is one of resilience, then she embodies it. There's a lot that we can learn from her story, most importantly that we must speak up boldly. There are more than enough resources for citizen and foreigner alike, so we are free to welcome immigrants to our land without fear.

10

Reconciliation

If we were reconciled to God through the death of his Son while we were still enemies, now that we have been reconciled, how much more certain is it that we will be saved by his life?
—ROMANS 5:10

I remember going to confession in our Catholic parish in Guatemala. As a little girl, I stood grimly outside a little wooden booth, staring at my scuffed shoes and reflecting guiltily on all the mean things I'd done to my brother and sister that week. When it was my turn, I'd step into the booth and kneel. When the priest prompted me, I would tell him of my childhood misdeeds, most of which involved disobeying my parents in one way or another. He'd tell me to repeat a memorized prayer a few times, and he'd speak words of absolution over me. I'd run out of the booth relieved and committed to being good.

I understood very little about this holy sacrament and its implications for life with God and our neighbors. In confession, sinners reconcile with God and the church for the wounds they have inflicted. Confession is a recognition that every time we sin, we hurt ourselves, others, and God, and things have to be made right. Sometimes it's called the sacrament of penance or confession, but I love the connotations of the word *reconciliation*, as in former enemies being made friends. In essence, reconciliation reflects immigrants' journey in the Bible: foreigners become citizens, strangers become family.

Starting from scratch

When I was eleven, my little sister Michelle started kindergarten. Out of all three of us, Michelle was the only one whose schooling took place entirely in the United States. One day in early September, I received a request to excuse me from my sixth-grade class to report to Ms. Lee's class in the kindergarten wing of our elementary school. I didn't know why, but I arrived to find my mother in the classroom, standing with my little sister at the teacher's desk. There was relief on Ms. Lee's smiling face when she saw me. She had been struggling to communicate with my mother and hadn't found a bilingual adult to help with translation.

"Honey, would you tell your mom that she needs to have your sister's hearing tested? She doesn't hear or respond to her name when I call on her. I think she might have hearing loss."

I was surprised and couldn't quite believe it, but I told my mother what the teacher had said: "Dice que Misha no contesta cuando la llama porque es sorda. Quiere que la lleve al médico." (She says Misha doesn't answer when she's called on because she's deaf. She wants you to take her to the doctor.)

My mother was incredulous. She was a nurse and had never once suspected my sister was deaf, as I had mistranslated, or had any amount of hearing loss, as Ms. Lee had actually stated. Thinking she knew exactly what was behind this problem, my mother began to scold my frightened sister in her limited English. "Michelle! Why don't you listen to the teacher? She calls you and—"

"Michelle?" Ms. Lee interrupted. "The class roster says her name is Lindsay."

"That's her first name, but Michelle is her middle name," I explained, "but we've never called her Lindsay—only Misha or Michelle."

"Oh! Then that's the problem. Does she know her name is Lindsay too?" she asked.

I shrugged and translated for my mother, whose countenance lightened once she registered the misunderstanding. They reached an agreement: Ms. Lee would call my sister Michelle in class, and my mother would teach her that her first name was Lindsay to avoid such situations in the future. I went back to my class, and my mother took Michelle home now that her half-day kindergarten was complete.

Recently I related this incident to my sister, who is now a speech pathologist in the public school system and works with children with special needs. She didn't remember it, but we both noted how such misunderstandings, if not resolved, can lead to immigrant children with limited English proficiency being misplaced in special education classes. It's a fact that there's a disproportionate number of English language learners in special education classes. Studies have shown that most mainstream teachers receive little to no training in how to distinguish a language acquisition issue from a learning disability. Often, teachers assume that a student's fluent social language—the simple, informal language that students use when they talk to their peers—translates into the same fluency in academic language. But on average it takes approximately seven to ten years to acquire academic-level English and only one to three years to acquire social language.[1]

That day we saved Michelle from unnecessary hearing and speech evaluations. Thanks to the good education my parents had provided for me in Guatemala, I knew enough Spanish vocabulary to translate for my mother. I didn't know at the time how significant it was. During the first few years we lived in the United States, I often participated in resolving adult problems for my parents because of their lack of fluency in English. It was just my reality, and I never gave it a second thought. I talked to insurance companies, bank tellers, travel agents, doctors, and customer service representatives. I read newspaper and magazine articles and communicated the gist to my mother. This experience isn't mine alone. As I've gotten to know other first- and second-generation immigrants, I've learned that we share this experience. We become our parents' assistants and translators, helping these once-independent adults navigate the new world in which they live. Language is easier to learn if you're a child whose only job is to go to school and learn English.

Tennent, a missiologist and the president of Asbury Theological Seminary, has noted in his research that Asian and Latinx immigrants are more likely either to be or become Christians than native-born North Americans are. As such, immigrants represent the greatest hope of renewal for a North American church in decline.[3] Their own journey also leads them to be reconciled to God.

It seems so appropriate that a church born out of a God born to a humble Middle Eastern family in a conquered and subjugated land would find hope from mostly poor immigrants. That the future of the church in North America would be wedded to the future of its immigrants—that their blessing and thriving would be stitched together—seems apt given that our Savior declared, "Love each other just as I have loved you" (John 15:12).

Finding myself in John 4

But beyond giving me a family in his church, Jesus practices a holistic relationship ethic—much like the Samaritan woman, whom Jesus sees and knows as a woman, as a Samaritan, and as a fallen person (John 4). Jesus reveals his identity as Messiah to this unnamed woman, and she is the first to spread the gospel to her own people, the Samaritans. She departs joyfully, leaving even her water container behind at the well.

Jesus transforms her life, her view of herself, and perhaps even her calling. But she remains both a Samaritan and a woman. Interestingly, John, the gospel writer, chooses to disclose both her gender and her ethnicity and even provides a brief note on the ethnic rift between Jews and Samaritans (see John 4:9). These details suggest that the Samaritan woman's social identity is a central component of the story, not an afterthought.

The Samaritan woman is remade by the gospel—she finds her identity and purpose in her encounter with Christ and embarks on a journey to be like him. Yet she no more ceases to be a Samaritan than she ceases to be female. Her social identity is a factor in how she receives the gospel and in how she spreads it. Jesus specifically references her identity as a Samaritan, and as a Samaritan, she becomes an emissary of hope to her own people. Her social location remains an essential part of the story. The testimony she gives—"he told me everything I have ever done" (see John 4:29)—suggests that she feels deeply known and accepted by Jesus as she is.

For years, my goal was to become a mature Christian. I was surrounded by American Christians I loved and respected, and I thought "Christian" was the only identity that mattered. I firmly believed that Jesus did not care that I was a woman, or a Guatemalan, or an immigrant, or a bicultural person. Despite how those identities have shaped and, at times, marginalized me, I thought I somehow shed them when I became a Christian. I now believe that Jesus meets me at all those intersections, just as he did for the Samaritan woman.

I am a Christian. But I have not ceased to be Latina, Guatemalan, an immigrant, and a woman. Because I now accept those overlapping identities, I'm free to love my whole self in all its God-authored complexity.

11

The Holy Family

Our Refugee Savior and a Love with No Limits

An angel from the Lord appeared to Joseph in a dream and said, "Get up. Take the child and his mother and escape to Egypt."
—MATTHEW 2:13

Tucked in the middle of Matthew's second chapter is a short narrative not told in any other gospel. It's the story of a dramatic incident in the life of the holy family. We learn that after Jesus' birth, his parents had to flee with their child to Egypt.

> When the magi had departed, an angel from the Lord appeared to Joseph in a dream and said, "Get up. Take the child and his mother and escape to Egypt. Stay there un-

> til I tell you, for Herod will soon search for the child in order to kill him." Joseph got up and, during the night, took the child and his mother to Egypt. He stayed there until Herod died. This fulfilled what the Lord had spoken through the prophet: I have called my son out of Egypt. (Matthew 2:13-15)

Herod, the all-powerful king, is troubled at the coming of King Jesus, but he is unable to destroy him. God sees this humble family, and God's hand is upon them and not upon the rulers of the nations. Frustrated and determined to find and murder the child Jesus, Herod unleashes his vengeance by slaughtering the children of his own people.[1] But throughout the story, God's divine eye is evident in the preservation of the holy family and the fulfillment of Old Testament prophecies.

It's difficult to read that story and not think of the bands of immigrants arriving at the southern U.S. border, on the shores of Greece, and at the ports of entry of other European nations. Sometimes they are parents and children fleeing their homelands, and other times they are minors traveling on their own. Like the holy family, they seek refuge from violence and terror. There may not be a ruthless Herod chasing them, but there are repressive governments, wars, and gangs. There are corrupt police and border and military officers who persecute rather than protect them.

It is likely intentional on the part of Matthew, the gospel writer, to introduce early on in his account the foreign magi. Those we frequently call wise men were probably astronomers who, in contrast to Herod, come to worship and bring gifts to the child Jesus. They follow a star from their distant homeland so they can see him. In King Herod, we see paranoia, fear, and resistance to God; in these foreigners we see obedience to the divine will.[2]

It is an irony that is repeated throughout the book of Matthew. Leaders of the Jews—Herod, the Pharisees, the Sadducees, the chief priests—reject Jesus. Those on the outside, like the magi, receive him.[3]

Imaginary lines

Herod sees Jesus as a threat to his own leadership. He has heard about this child who would one day be king and usurp him, and he decides that Jesus must be found and murdered. In modern terms, we would say that Jesus and his parents are refugees. The legal definition of a refugee is a person who flees from his or her home country to seek refuge elsewhere because of persecution—or a well-founded fear of persecution—on account of race, religion, nationality, political opinion, or membership in a particular social group.[4]

It's important to clarify that in the ancient world, borders as we conceive of them today did not exist, and as a result, neither did refugee status. To be sure, there were separate nations, such as Egypt, Syria, and Israel. But there were no imaginary hard lines delineated on maps, or visas and passports required to live in or travel to a foreign land. Joseph and Mary simply gathered their child and fled. It's very likely that they sold the valuable gifts of gold, frankincense, and myrrh the magi had given them and used the funds to pay for their travel to the safety of a land far away, where the evil hand of Herod could not reach them.

We who live in the twenty-first century assume that borders and walls have always been a natural part of life and are necessary. We appreciate the clear separation that says that this land is mine and that land is yours. But this perspective was not always universally accepted—in fact, historically speaking, it's relatively new. Borders, as we understand them, arose after the Thirty Years' War, which took place from 1618 to 1648; all the European powers participated in this war, and it resulted in the deaths of a quarter of the European population. Subsequently, the treaties of Westphalia introduced the idea of territorial sovereignty, shown clearly on maps, in order to establish who had the right to make decisions over what land—particularly when it came to determining which Christian tradition, Catholic or Protestant, each nation would follow. Rather than constantly falling victim to religious wars, people had the freedom to migrate to a sovereign state where their Christian faith expression was practiced. By the twentieth century, these now more established European sovereign states created a system of passports and visas to establish citizenship and, ironically, to restrict the movement of people.[5]

Many historians and cartographers dispute the idea that borders are natural and essential; instead, many believe that it's the movement of people that's natural, and that borders and the restriction of movements between them exist to control and limit access to resources.[6] Furthermore, these scholars assert that it's the borders themselves that produce the violence which surrounds them. In other words, borders might actually create the very challenges that have come to be seen as their trademarks, including creating opportunities for criminality:

the trafficking of people, goods, drugs, weapons, and money across them. Professor Reece Jones reinforces this point: "The hardening of borders through new security practices is the source of the violence, not a response to it."[7]

Although it may seem counterintuitive, the "hardening" of borders and the building of walls actually make nations *less* secure, not more so. Borders actually increase criminal activity and place people in situations that make them vulnerable to exploitation and death.

A secure border, not a closed one

Of course, none of this means that we should travel back in time to the end of the Thirty Years' War to undo the creation of sovereign states and borders. But it does raise some important questions for followers of Jesus: How does God see the people who come to borders, seeking admission? How do we respond to closed borders that especially harm the world's poor? What is the responsibility of the church versus that of the state to those who ask for admission to a country?

At least part of the answer lies in 1 John 3:17-18, in which the writer puts it this way: "But if a person has material possessions and sees a brother or sister in need and that person doesn't care—how can the love of God remain in him? Little children, let's not love with words or speech but with action and truth."

Followers of Jesus must weigh the violence against God's image-bearers, violence created by closed borders, with their own fears about national security. We need not travel too far back in time to find that U.S. and Canadian borders were once porous but secure. They were *not* heavily guarded; this was a fact for most of the twentieth century and would change only if and when these states were at war with any of their neighbors.[8] This approach, which lasted into the latter half of the twentieth century, was a more humane way to deal with immigrants in need, and it created a win-win scenario that accommodated complementary interests: migrants, primarily from the Global South, provided a needed labor force. North American countries, with their shrinking and aging labor forces, provided safety and a labor market for migrants.[9] Loving our neighbors in truth and action, as John prescribes, demands that we ask our legislators to return to these times when borders were less like impenetrable walls and more like gates that swung both ways.

While it's true that churches don't have to make decisions that nations must, as voting citizens in a republic, church members do have the right to influence legislators according to their values. Our values as Christians should always reflect our allegiance to Christ above all. For the Christian there is no conflict in voting for legislators who support humane immigration policies and porous but secure borders.

It's uncomfortable, and maybe even frightening, for many of us to consider having porous borders, especially in a time when terrorism abounds around the globe. Yet Christians are not called to value the false sense of security created by closed borders and walls. We are called to trust in God and to love our neighbors, particularly our neighbors in need. Closed borders in North America are not directed toward an existing threat of invasion by a foreign army but toward poor economic immigrants seeking opportunities and toward refugees fleeing for their very lives. Hardened borders are designed to prevent the movement of the world's poor—a people whom God says Christians should care for and not harm.

The prophet Isaiah reminds us that the fasting which God desires is sharing our bread with the hungry and bringing the homeless poor into our houses (Isaiah 58:7). What does sharing our bread look like today? What does bringing the homeless poor into our homes mean? We could say that sharing our bread is sharing the opportunities in North American labor markets. And perhaps bringing the poor into our houses means welcoming immigrants in need into our countries, just as Egypt welcomed Mary, Joseph, and the child Jesus.

We in the Western church know next to nothing about the holy family's sojourn in Egypt, but the Egyptian Coptic Church has marked several places where the family is believed to have stayed. In those locations the church has built shrines and churches to commemorate the family's time there. We know the holy family found refuge in Egypt and were not turned away. For a short time, they made their lives in the safety of Egypt.

When Herod died, Joseph had another dream that prompted the family's return to their own land. There they settled and thus fulfilled the prophecy of a savior from Nazareth near the Sea of Galilee.

La Posada sin Fronteras

Every year from December 16 to 24, Las Posadas is celebrated in many Latin American countries. Roughly translated, *posada* means "inn" or "shelter." Las Posadas recalls the events in Luke's gospel leading up to Jesus' birth. It's a Catholic Christian observance with a sung liturgy that's performed on the streets rather than in church.

A posada begins with a street procession that reenacts Mary and Joseph's search for shelter at an inn. Those playing the protagonists of the story, Mary and Joseph, are dressed in costume and carry candles as they follow a prescribed route, knocking on doors. At each door they ask, through special Posadas songs, for room at the inn. In rural areas, Mary may even ride on a donkey.

The verses of the song are sung alternately by those outside and those inside the home. This creates a sung dialogue between Joseph and an innkeeper.

Joseph:

En el nombre del cielo	In the name of heaven
os pido posada,	I ask you for shelter,
pues no puede andar	for my beloved wife
mi esposa amada.	can go no farther.

Innkeeper:

Aquí no es mesón	This is not an inn
sigan adelante,	Get on with you,
yo no puedo abrir,	I cannot open the door,
no sea algún tunante.	you might be a criminal.

Many people from the community follow behind, singing along with them. The neighbors participating in the Posada open their doors, and each one purposefully sings their refusal to Mary and Joseph. Only at the very end of the route does a designated household finally allow Mary and Joseph to come in. There, too, is a party with Bible readings, food, and piñatas for the children. Now that the holy family has found their welcome, it is time to celebrate.

Las Posadas is a beautiful Advent tradition, and a beloved part of Christmas celebrations in many Latinx communities. It is also one that ministers and immigration advocates have begun to use to represent the lack of hospitality at the U.S.-Mexico border. Their version is called La Posada sin Fronteras: Shelter without Borders.

La Posada sin Fronteras uses the exact same songs as the traditional Posadas liturgy. But rather than walking through a neighborhood and knocking on doors, immigration advocates, faith leaders, immigrants, and other supporters gather on both sides of the U.S.-Mexico border. There they are watched carefully by Border Patrol as they begin their reenactment of the journey of Mary and Joseph. The group on the Mexican side represents Mary and Joseph asking for shelter, while those on the U.S. side play the innkeeper, who repeatedly rejects their request for shelter. It's a reenactment that "contextualizes the bitter drama" of displaced immigrants, writes Ched Myers in *Our God Is Undocumented*. And it brings participants inside the sacred story of God struggling to enter an inhospitable world.[10]

Joseph (those on the Mexican side of the border wall, representing immigrants):

No seas inhumano,	Don't be inhuman,
tennos caridad,	have mercy on us,

que el Dios de los cielos	God in heaven
te lo premiará.	will reward you.

Innkeeper (those on the U.S. side of the wall, representing the U.S. Border Patrol and, by extension, U.S. citizens):

Ya se pueden ir	You can go now
y no molestar	and don't bother me,
porque si me enfado	because if I become angry
los voy a apalear.	I'm going to beat you up.

This uncomfortable liturgy, set in a location where so much violence takes place, removes the sanitized romanticism of modern-day Christmas observances. It recalls the stark realities faced by Mary and Joseph on that night long ago. Most of us like to imagine that we would have welcomed Mary and Joseph into our homes and provided shelter. But La Posada sin Fronteras reminds us of all the obstacles that stand in a migrant's path and that are supported by our tax dollars: the wall at the border, the drones, the guardhouses, the rubber bullets, and the vigilant and heavily armed Border Patrol. Remembering these things keeps us firmly rooted in reality: That we likely would not have welcomed them. That in the liturgy, we are the hard-hearted innkeeper who threatens Joseph with assault.

I've never visited the Middle East, but I imagine that its climate is not unlike the one in the twin border cities of Nogales, Arizona, and Nogales, Sonora, one of the many locations where La Posada sin Fronteras takes place. It's not difficult to imagine Mary and Joseph trudging along the dusty, dry wilderness of Ambos Nogales, as the twin cities are sometimes called, there where the border wall stretches for what seems like an eternity. There the holy parents plod along, seeking shelter, a safe place to find rest and for Mary to give birth to the Son of God. There, we imagine, they know that their God sees them, and they pray that someone will have mercy on them in their desperate situation.

Of course, their story in the Posadas liturgy has the most joyful of endings. The innkeeper eventually has a change of heart. He finally recognizes Joseph and opens his door to welcome them inside:

Entren santos peregrinos, peregrinos,	Enter holy pilgrims, pilgrims,
reciban este rincón	receive this corner
no de esta pobre morada	not this poor dwelling
sino de mi corazón.	but my heart.
Esta noche es de alegría	Tonight is for joy,
de gusto y de regocijo	for gladness and rejoicing,
porque hospedaremos aquí	for tonight we will give lodging
a la Madre de Dios Hijo.	to the mother of God the Son.

Those who participate in La Posada sin Fronteras know that our story has no such happy ending—so far, at least. The wall remains. A militarized border remains. The door remains closed. There is no innkeeper having a sudden epiphany that it is the mother of God herself to whom he denies hospitality. But La Posada sin Fronteras is reenacted each year as an act of faith and hope. It requires hope to act out a story with a happy ending when the story they are living doesn't yet have such an ending—the participants are trusting that God is at work even in things they don't see or understand. Their hopes echo the book of Hebrews, which puts it this way: "Faith is the reality of what we hope for, the proof of what we don't see" (Hebrews 11:1).

Still, the participants throw candy over the wall to each other, showering one another with sweets. Often they can't see one another. But they know that God sees the groups gathered on each side. Together they commit to bring the wall down in their lifetimes and never to internalize its message in their hearts.[11]

One family in Christ

When I lived in Kazakhstan, I learned the value of my little blue U.S. passport. As a teacher there, I met many Russians and Kazakhs who longed to migrate to Canada, the United States, and western Europe—not because they didn't love their own countries but because they lacked the opportunities to improve their lives. I felt blessed to have been able to get residency and citizenship in the United States, and I never questioned the political and global forces that had created such unequal conditions in the world.

The valid critiques my Kazakh friends had of the United States would often upset me. In conversations in which they shared their criticisms of my adopted country, I'd find myself clinging ever more strongly to my American identity.

But over time, I began to realize that my identity is not found in the color of my passport or the place I reside. The

Bible says that our identities are in Christ: the refugee God whose love knew no limits and lived a life committed to justice and peace. The book of Acts reminds us, "In God we live, move, and exist" (Acts 17:28). In other words, our true "place" is in Jesus, not on a map with borders. We live inside God, not within a particular nation.

I believe firmly that in God's family, there are no borders. We who belong to Christ are all one family in Christ. The story of Christmas—of foreigners and poor shepherds gathering to welcome and celebrate their newborn king—is a complete reversal of expectations. Our Savior, who became a refugee with his humble parents, grew up to have no place to lay his head: this truth is a reversal too.

Jesus reminds us in Matthew 25 that when we welcome foreigners and others in vulnerable situations, we welcome him.

It was God disguised as Ruth who arrived in Bethlehem as a poor widow. It was God whom Boaz welcomed into his fields, and God whom the community welcomed and loved as one of their own.

It was God disguised as Abraham and Sarah who was driven to Egypt by a famine and then suffered the suspicion and abuse to which all immigrants are subjected.

It was God disguised as the foreign enslaved girl Hagar who was mistreated and driven to the desert to seek liberation.

It was God disguised as Joseph who suffered unjust enslavement and imprisonment, spending years wondering if he would see his family again.

It was God disguised as a Syrophoenician woman with a demon-possessed daughter who pled for wholeness and mercy.

And it was God who came to us long ago in a manger, teaching us by example how to love one another and care for the poor and marginalized. Though the world may ignore the afflictions of immigrants, God sees clearly, cares deeply, and acts decisively in Christ. Though they are marginalized in the world, immigrants are significant in the eyes of God.

You are the God who sees, Hagar said, and the same God who saw Hagar sees us. Indeed, the question is not whether God will see and hear and welcome us. The question is whether we will see and hear and welcome God. Will we live out the radical and subversive hospitality that Jesus modeled for us?

Ideas for Action and Reflection

People frequently ask me what they can do in response to the issues presented in this book. How can they get involved in advocacy for or relationships with immigrants and refugees? It's an excellent question. Once we become aware of our immigrant neighbors, all Christians should ask: "What do I do now?"

Prayer and reflection

The first step should always be reflection and prayer. I encourage you to prayerfully consider these questions:

1. Where did you learn your views on immigration? Are your views of immigration *primarily* informed by the Bible and Jesus' teachings? Or are they informed by political

rhetoric, your family, your peers, or the media? It's critical to be honest with yourself in God's presence. Only the Holy Spirit can transform our views and align them with biblical values. Getting involved with immigrants out of sympathy for their plight is not necessarily bad, but the transformation that God desires is one of mutuality. You love your neighbors in need *and* you are transformed by the Spirit. Figuring out what you think about immigrants and immigration is critical *before* you engage the issue or immigrants themselves. Building real community and solidarity with immigrants requires nothing less.

2. Do you have any relationships with immigrants? Not transactional relationships, like the woman who cleans your house, the man who mows your lawn, or the server at your favorite Mexican restaurant. Are you involved with immigrants in close relationships *as equals*? Immigrants are all around you: in your workplace, at your university, in your church, and at your children's school. Consider practicing the spiritual discipline of hospitality and being intentional in initiating a relationship with an immigrant or immigrant family. This act of hospitality could include having them over to your house for dinner; accepting an invitation to their home; working on a church event together; or attending a PTA meeting or children's sporting event. Humility and intentionality are required on your part to make sure this relationship is mutual. This effort will likely be awkward and require perseverance on all parts, but relationships are key to the immigration issue, because it's fundamentally about people.

3. Are you willing to speak up and stand up for immigrants? This question does not mean that you need to become a professional who advocates for immigration policy changes with politicians. Are you willing to stand up to family and friends who espouse anti-immigrant views that disparage the image of God in immigrants? You do not need to convince them, of course, because only God's Spirit can bring about such a change. But it's important to be willing to speak up to defend the dignity of immigrants. This can be done gently—by asking questions, seeking to find common ground, and offering correction where there is misinformation. Perhaps you won't persuade your family and friends, but ultimately as Christians we have a duty to love our neighbors. Sometimes that requires the courage to simply speak up for them.
4. Consider the language you use when you talk about immigrants. Language matters because it shapes reality. You may have noticed that in this book, I use language that humanizes immigrants. For example, I refer to people who don't have the legal authorization to be in the country as undocumented or unauthorized immigrants. Processes can be legal or illegal, but people cannot be. Examine the language you use and the language you hear around you. Does it respect the dignity of immigrants as image-bearers of God? Does it disparage them and strip them of their humanity?
5. Finally, pray for immigrants and refugees, asking God for discernment in how you can serve the community.

Political advocacy

This might sound scary, but one of the easiest and most effective ways that you can serve your immigrant neighbors in need is to vote. If you are in the United States, you live in a constitutional republic. And if you live in Canada, you live in a federal parliamentary system under a constitutional monarch. In both cases, you have the power to vote and influence legislation on behalf of immigrants. Remember, your representatives in Congress or Parliament work for you!

You can contact your legislators to thank them for supporting legislation for immigrants and immigration reform, or you can ask for their support on a particular issue. Some ways you can contact them are through letters, through phone calls (most effective!), and by tagging them on social media. If you're in the United States, call the United States Capitol switchboard (202-224-3121) to find out who your legislators are and to be connected to their office. You will be asked for your name, address, and the reason for your call. Use a short script like this one (or others found online) when you call:

> Hi! I'm [first and last name] from [city, state]. I'm calling to urge [legislator name] to secure a legislative solution for immigration reform [or Dreamers or keeping immigrant families together].
>
> As a person of faith, I am deeply troubled and concerned by the lack of protection immigrants have in our country.
>
> I encourage [legislator name] to stand with the immigrant community and continue our country's legacy of welcoming immigrants. Thank you for your time.

Set a reminder on your calendar to call once a month. The loudest group of voices speaking into the immigration debate are anti-immigrant; be sure to let your voice be counted in support of immigrants.

Visit immigrants in detention

Every year, hundreds of thousands of people are detained in immigration jails across the country. These are mothers, fathers, brothers, sisters, sons, daughters, and individuals who are often isolated and held in prisons far from their families and communities.

A conversation with a detained person can provide support and friendship while deepening your perspective on the realities of the system. Visitation programs can arrange your visit, guide you through the entire process, provide in-depth training, and address specific questions or concerns pertaining to your local detention center.

If you can listen and hold a conversation, you have all the requirements needed for visiting immigrants being held in ICE detention prisons. Prayerfully consider this possibility for yourself, your community, or both, and learn more about detention visitation at Freedom for Immigrants (https://www.freedomforimmigrants.org/visitor-volunteer-resources/).

Give to immigrant legal service providers

Much of the help needed to serve and protect immigrants is in the form of providing them immigration legal services. Unlike those in the criminal justice system, immigrants are not guaranteed an attorney in federal court unless they pay for it themselves or they find pro bono legal help. These are excellent nonprofit organizations working to provide such services:

- World Relief (www.worldrelief.org). World Relief, my employer, is a Christian nonprofit that empowers local churches to directly serve immigrants and leads its field offices in providing legal services. Many of World Relief's twenty U.S. offices provide legal services to immigrant communities. You can designate your gift to "immigrant legal services."
- RAICES (www.raicestexas.org). RAICES is a nonprofit agency that promotes justice by providing free and low-cost legal services to underserved immigrant children, families, and refugees in Texas.
- Kids in Need of Defense (www.supportkind.org). KIND is a nonprofit agency that provides immigration legal services to children. Their mission is to ensure that no child appears in immigration court without high-quality legal representation and to protect children's rights and well-being when they migrate alone.
- Al Otro Lado (https://alotrolado.org). Al Otro Lado is a California-based nonprofit that provides direct legal services to indigent deportees, migrants, and refugees in Tijuana, Mexico.

Other resources for Bible study or information on immigration

Much harm is done to the immigrant community with the spread of false information. Think carefully and double-check the source of any articles, blog posts, memes, or social media posts before you make them, whether they are in support of immigration or against it. The following websites are the most reliable sources for accurate information on immigrants and immigration:

- American Immigration Council (www.americanimmigrationcouncil.org)
- The National Immigration Forum (www.immigrationforum.org)
- Migration Policy Institute (www.migrationpolicy.org)
- Refugee Council USA (www.rcusa.org)

World Relief provides additional free resources for Christians seeking to learn more about the immigration issue at Welcoming the Stranger (www.welcomingthestranger.com) and its primary website (https://worldrelief.org/church-leaders-resources-download/). These include:

- *Church Leader's Guide to Immigration*: addresses the most common legal, biblical, and practical questions that pastors and church leaders may have; and
- *Discovering and Living God's Heart for Immigrants: A Guide to Welcoming the Stranger*: a downloadable curriculum suitable for a small group or adult Sunday school class.

You can also read this book with a book club, Sunday school class, or small group to provoke discussion, prayer, and reflection around this subject. Discussion questions for *The God Who Sees* appear in the next section and are also available at HeraldPress.com.

Discussion Questions

CHAPTER 1
Ruth and Naomi: A Blessed Alliance

1. Reflect on what you were taught about the book of Ruth. Who or what has been the traditional and dominant focus of the book? Or if you not yet read it, take time to read this short but important book of the Bible.
2. Have you ever heard the book of Ruth taught as the story of an immigrant who was welcomed into the family of God? If you haven't, why do you suppose that is? How could you bring this biblical perspective to your church community?
3. The book is called *Ruth*, but the biblical character who undergoes significant personal transformation in her relationship with God is Naomi. Reflect on Naomi's

change of heart. What contributes to her shift in perspective? How does her example speak to you?

4. Naomi is also the only Judean in the story who knows firsthand the experience of being an immigrant. Have you ever experienced being the foreigner or the outsider? How did you feel in that situation?
5. Ruth worked hard in the fields, doing work that many others did in her day. Immigrants in North America often do work that nobody else wants to do. Where do the immigrants in your community work? If you're not sure, consider researching this information.
6. Karen González ponders the fact that Judah would have missed many blessings had the nation rejected Ruth at the border. How might this story have been different for all involved if Ruth had been unable to migrate?

CHAPTER 2
Baptism

1. Have you or someone you know been baptized? What do you know or remember about this experience? If you have been baptized, what did it mean to you or to your family?
2. González recounts her own family's history with the Christian faith (p. 36). What do you know of your family's religious heritage? How has it contributed or not contributed to your own formation as a Christian?

3. On pages 39–41, González describes her first encounter with a Protestant church. Do you remember your first encounter with a Christian tradition different from your own? What was that experience like?
4. Were you surprised to learn that González and her family loved living in their native Guatemala and had never dreamed of emigrating? Why do you think this type of information is often left out of conversations on immigration?
5. Think of the immigrants you know. What do you know about their lives before migration? Besides the factors that pushed them to leave their country, what were the joys of their lives in their native lands? What memories do they cherish? Do you feel comfortable inviting them to reflect on these questions? If you don't have close relationships with immigrants, consider why that might be.

CHAPTER 3
Abraham: The Immigrant Father of Our Faith

1. Francisco was arrested while trying to be a good neighbor to others in his community. Does it surprise you to learn that doing the right thing can have terrible results? What do we learn about our laws through what happened to Francisco?
2. Have you ever thought of Abraham as an immigrant? Or as an immigrant who committed fraud while trafficking his wife? Why or why not?

3. How does hearing the full stories of Francisco and Abram/Abraham change your perspective on their respective crimes?
4. As a woman entering a foreign land, Sarah was uniquely vulnerable. In what ways are immigrant women more vulnerable than immigrant men?
5. How do we reconcile the fact that immigrants break the law when they cross the border with their whole story? How do you weigh this question of law against the question of what drove them to such measures?
6. Can you think of any U.S. or Canadian laws that, in your opinion, should be abolished or amended? Why do you think so?

CHAPTER 4
Communion

1. If you have ever celebrated communion, do you remember the first time you took communion? What was the experience like for you? What did it mean to you personally?
2. González shares that she distinctly remembers choosing to pursue her first communion and felt drawn toward God (p. 60). How do you recall being drawn to God before you committed your life to following Christ?
3. González mentions that, at eight years old, she was very aware that there was war, violence, and death around

her, causing her great fear and anxiety. Yet the adults in her life assumed she was oblivious to these happenings (pp. 60–65). Why do we often underestimate the understanding of children? How would you speak to a child about such events? How would you alleviate their fears?

4. Conversations around immigration often have to do with what draws immigrants to the United States or Canada and do not focus on the policies of nations like the United States that created the conditions which force people to leave their homelands. How can we promote discussion and awareness at this macro level? Why is it important for North Americans to understand these realities?
5. González tells the story of her attempt at protest in her high school (pp. 65–67), motivated by her feelings of betrayal and disillusionment at the U.S. government. What are some effective ways to engage children and adolescents in activism around issues they care about? What are some ways that adults can also engage and not feel powerless in the face of injustice?
6. González tells the story of Archbishop Oscar Romero and his costly decision to stand with those who were poor and oppressed in his native El Salvador. Why do you suppose that Romero's government was so threatened by his remembrance of those who had been killed? How does the gospel have implications beyond personal piety?

CHAPTER 5
Hagar: "The Foreign Thing" and the God Who Sees Her

1. What do you know about your own name and why it was given to you? Imagine how your experience within your family might have been different if you'd been called a general term like "Boy" or "Girl" or "Little One."
2. Have you heard sermons about Hagar? If not, consider why that might be. What do we learn about God by considering God's appearance to Hagar?
3. What similarities exist between the messenger of God appearing to Mary and Hagar?
4. On page 75, González says, "Hagar in the desert reminds all of us that the Spirit can be found in the places we least expect: with the poor, the outcasts, the enslaved people, the domestic help, and the foreigners." Can you think of examples of God's appearance to those the world would discard? How has God appeared to you?
5. González shares that her abuelita took pride in her work as a housekeeper, recognizing that all work has meaning and dignity. God engaged in the lowly work of creation too (p. 76). Does this knowledge change your perspective on domestic work? How so?
6. González describes *lo cotidiano*, the everyday, as the way her abuelita lived her faith in the ordinary tasks. How do you work out your faith in the ordinary?
7. González writes, "My abuelita contributed more than hard work to her new country; she brought the gift of

her faith, her theology of survival" (p. 77). We often focus on what immigrants take or the resources they receive, but we don't discuss the many things they bring. What do immigrants bring when they arrive at their adopted country? What do they have to offer?

8. How can you move from reading the Bible from the perspective of those in the dominant culture to that of those on the margins? Why is this an important shift?

CHAPTER 6
Confirmation

1. Has confirmation been part of your experience in churches? Was there a time that you "confirmed" your faith, even informally? How did you make your faith your own?
2. González recounts the experiences of her Afro-Guatemalan relatives who experience marginalization because of both race and ethnicity (pp. 84–85). Did this surprise you? Where have you encountered overlapping identities that marginalize people even further?
3. Were you familiar with remittances? Why do you think that women especially rely on remittances from their relatives working in the United States, Canada, and other Western nations?
4. González discusses "abuelita theology" and the faith passed down to her informally by her grandmother (pp. 86–87). How has faith been passed down to you? Or if

it wasn't, how do you intend to pass down your own faith to your children or others in the next generation?

5. On page 88, González tells us of her attempts at prayer as a new Christian. What did your first prayers sound like? What feelings or reactions arise as you recall those early conversations with God? Reflect on how you have grown in your prayer life since your early prayers.
6. González recalls reading a poem about the lost potential of those constrained by their condition and how this poem reminded her of her father, a man with a college education who had to do maintenance work after her family immigrated to the United States. How do you think immigrants cope with not being valued for their intellectual or professional gifts? What would you have done if you had been in her father's situation? Do you know any immigrants in a similar situation?

CHAPTER 7
Joseph: The Foreigner Who Blessed Egypt

1. González says that Ruth's and Joseph's stories have often been turned into fairy tales for children (p. 96). What happens when we make such romanticized adaptations to biblical stories? How does that affect our comprehension of the suffering of both Ruth and Joseph?
2. Had you ever thought of Joseph as a vulnerable foreigner who was the victim of multiple crimes and injustices in Egypt? Why or why not?

3. Were you surprised to learn that immigrants are more likely to become victims of crimes? How does that square with the fears people in North America have about immigrants themselves being criminals?
4. What caused the shift in Egypt from philoxenia (a love of immigrants) to xenophobia (a fear and hatred of immigrants)?
5. Where would you place yourself on the spectrum between xenophobia and philoxenia? How do you see yourself growing toward philoxenia?
6. How could you practically put into practice the spiritual discipline of hospitality as Richard Beck describes it (p. 106)?
7. How has Jesus come to you in disguise? Where have you encountered people in need, and how did you see Christ in them? How did you respond?

CHAPTER 8
Anointing the Sick

1. In your faith tradition, how do followers of Jesus respond to those who are sick and dying? Is there an expectation of a divine healing? Or an acceptance that God is in control of all outcomes? How have you processed the illnesses of those around you in terms of your faith and God's healing power?
2. What did you know about family-based immigration before you read this chapter? Were you surprised to

learn that only certain relatives are eligible? Did that change your perspective on immigration sponsorship?

3. González shares common stereotypes about Latina women (p. 113). How have your experiences with immigrants contradicted the stereotypes you have heard about them?
4. In Guatemala, it's a common belief that telling a sick person their diagnosis and prognosis will affect the person's will to live and minimize their fight for life (pp. 116–17). What beliefs exist in your community around sickness and death?
5. What visible signs like anointing the sick with oil have you performed in your faith practice? What do you think is the value or lack thereof of such signs?
6. What do you think about anointing being the last sacred rite people receive in their lives? Would such a sign bring you comfort?

CHAPTER 9
The Syrophoenician Woman: The Foreigner with Sass

1. What has been your interpretation of Jesus' encounter with the Syrophoenician woman in Mark 7:24–30?
2. This story makes many readers of Scripture uncomfortable. Do other biblical stories make you uncomfortable or confuse you? How do you resolve those tensions?

3. What similarities and differences do you see between the Syrophoenician woman's story and Alejandra's story?
4. Were you surprised to learn that Central America's gang problem originated in the United States? How can Western nations address the macro-level forces that drive immigration?
5. González writes that "out of all the immigration solutions available, asylum is one of the most difficult to get" (p. 130). If that is so, why do you suppose so many North American politicians and their supporters fear allowing immigrants at the U.S.-Mexico border to apply for asylum?
6. What do you think about the Syrophoenician woman's response? Would you speak to Jesus in such a way? What does Jesus' response to the woman reveal about him?

CHAPTER 10
Reconciliation

1. How did you first learn about confession and repentance? How did you feel about them?
2. How do you think immigrant children cope with language acquisition difficulties? Why do teachers sometimes assume language acquisition issues are actually learning disabilities?
3. How would you feel if you had to rely on your child or someone else's child to help you navigate the world?

What impact do you think this communication work has on immigrant children?

4. González explains the conflict and confusion of living with her parents' values at home and with other values at school. This created a divide between her and the adults in her family (pp. 141–46). Had you ever considered the losses that immigrant parents face in raising their children in another country and culture? How would you deal with such conflicts? How would you want your children to relate to you and their family's cultural background?
5. González discusses the challenge of not feeling fully Guatemalan and not being fully North American, of not belonging fully in either place. She also describes having found belonging in the family of God. How have you found a sense of belonging in God's family?
6. Are there social identities you possess that have shaped how you received the gospel? How have they affected you?

CHAPTER 11
The Holy Family: A Refugee Savior and a Love with No Limits

1. What did you know about the history of borders before reading this chapter? How does this chapter affect your view of your own nation's borders?

2. Does having porous rather than militarized borders frighten you in any way? Why or why not? How can you as a Christian deal with this fear?
3. Have you ever heard of or participated in a Posada? What traditions does your faith community practice that were perhaps inspired by Scripture but aren't an exact reflection of it?
4. Had you ever considered what you might have done if Mary and Joseph had knocked on your door? How do you feel about being identified with the innkeeper who denies hospitality to Mary and Joseph?
5. González says that the participants in La Posada sin Fronteras "are trusting that God is at work even in things they don't see or understand" (p. 160). How are you encouraged by that scriptural truth?
6. How is your identity as a U.S. or Canadian citizen—or any other nationality—separate from your identity as a Christian? Which identity shapes you most fundamentally?

Acknowledgments

Before I wrote this book, I didn't know that writing it would be a communal effort as much as it would be a solitary activity. I'm ever so grateful for my editor, Valerie Weaver-Zercher, who gently encouraged my writing, rewriting, and editing. I used to believe in great writers, but now I only believe in great editors! Valerie made this book what it is—she believed in it and its message from the beginning and improved upon it in so many ways. Her patience with me as a new writer who missed nearly every deadline cannot be underestimated. I'm also grateful for the entire team at Herald Press: you brought this book to life, and I'm enormously in your debt.

Without my family who embarked on this journey of immigration, there would be no story to tell. Writing this story has been hard emotional work, but it's nothing compared to the work my parents put into integrating into a new culture, learning a new language, and seeking a better life for their children. Reentering those memories helped me to understand your struggles and your sacrifices just a little bit—I love you and am deeply indebted to you. I'm equally thankful to my sister, Michelle, and my brother, Jorge, who not only celebrated the birthing of this book but also helped my failing memory as I struggled to write it. You read parts, offered yourselves as resources, brainstormed book launch parties, and encouraged me all along the way. Most of all, you understand this book like no one else because you shared in the joy and the losses of the journey with me. I love you!

I have a wonderful community of friends who loved and supported me through this process. I'm especially thankful for all the group texts and conversations I shared with Candace Kim and Laura Depp Corcorran: you listened patiently to my anxious freak-outs about writing and helped me with the emotional processing that memoirs require. Most of all, you loved and cared for me as you always do, and I don't know what I would do without you. My friends Beth and Dan Watkins were invaluable research assistants and conversation partners as we got ice cream nearly every week last summer and discussed all things immigration! I still have several of your books, and I'm so thankful for your friendship. Thank you to Derek and Lisa Engdahl, who were invaluable mentors and friends as I began the process of reconnecting to my roots and rediscovering my identity as an immigrant. The two of you helped me to let go of the many things holding me back from my identity in Christ, and I'm thankful for you. So many friends have been part of bringing this book to life that it's impossible to name all of you, but I'm thankful to you all.

The publishing world is not for the faint of heart, and I could have never survived it without the support of my wonderful writing group. I'm grateful to these women, and especially to Ruthie Johnson, Heather Caliri, Andi Cumbo-Floyd, and Cara Meredith: you read early chapters of this book that were simply awful and provided very helpful feedback that made it better. Thank you for your honesty and your editing and revising gifts. You encouraged me to keep writing when I wanted to crawl into a ball and die.

There are many Latinas in my life who have provided guidance and encouragement. Thank you, Carolina Hinojosa-Cisneros, Sandy Ovalle, Kristy Robinson, Sandra Van Opstal, Inez Velázquez-McBryde, Kat Armas, and Mayra Macedo-Nolan. You have all modeled lives of love and service to our community, and my life is better for having met you.

Finally, I want to thank my colleagues at World Relief. Matt Soerens, you have taught me so much about advocating for immigrants and refugees with grace and truth. Patti Chiriboga-Roby and Kjerstin Lewis, you taught me nearly everything I know about immigration legal work—thank you for your tireless effort on behalf of immigrants. Thank you to my beloved Human Resources team, especially Kathleen Leslie and Janelle Fenyes: you have heard me talk about this book for months on end and have encouraged and celebrated the process without telling me to shut up and get back to work!

And of course, thank you to my three little nieces—Anya, Sasha, and Elena—who believe so much in my talent for writing that they want the next book dedicated to them. I love you, girls!

I would never have finished this book if not for the help and generosity of many people. Thank you to everyone who made it a reality.

Notes

Chapter 1

1 Tim Keller, "What Is Biblical Justice?" *Relevant Magazine*, August 23, 2012, https://relevantmagazine.com/god/practical-faith/what-biblical-justice.

2 Megan McKenna, *Not Counting Women and Children: Neglected Stories from the Bible* (Maryknoll, NY: Orbis Books, 2002), 109.

3 "Cultivating Fear: The Vulnerability of Immigrant Farmworkers in the US to Sexual Violence and Sexual Assault," Human Rights Watch, May 15, 2012, https://www.hrw.org/report/2012/05/15/cultivating-fear/vulnerability-immigrant-farmworkers-us-sexual-violence-and-sexual.

4 McKenna, *Not Counting Women and Children*, 109.

5 Carolyn Custis James, "The Blessed Alliance," *Youth Worker*, September 18, 2012, https://www.youthworker.com/articles/the-blessed-alliance-men-and-women-working-together-for-good/.

6 McKenna, *Not Counting Women and Children*, 109.

7 Arthur Waskow, "If the Biblical Ruth Came to America Today," May 21, 2012, https://theshalomcenter.org/content/if-biblical-ruth-came-america-today.

8 "Refugees and Asylum," U.S. Citizenship and Immigration Services, last modified November 12, 2015, www.uscis.gov/humanitarian/refugees-asylum.

9 "Family of U.S. Citizens," U.S. Citizenship and Immigration Services, last modified March 23, 2018, www.uscis.gov/family/family-us-citizens.

Chapter 3

1 M. Daniel Carroll R., *Christians at the Border: Immigration, the Church, and the Bible* (Grand Rapids, MI: Baker Academic, 2008), 73.

2 Wilda C. Gafney, *Womanist Midrash: A Reintroduction to the Women of the Torah and the Throne* (Louisville, KY: Westminster John Knox Press, 2017), 22.

3 "What Is Human Trafficking?" Anti-Slavery International, accessed August 8, 2018, https://www.antislavery.org/slavery-today/human-trafficking/.

4 Maurice Harris, "Abraham, Sarah and the Arizona Immigration Law," *Oregonian*, May 3, 2010, https://www.oregonlive.com/opinion/index.ssf/2010/05/abraham_sarah_and_the_arizona.html.

5 Deborah Bonello and Erin Siegal McIntyre, "Is Rape the Price to Pay for Migrant Women Chasing the American Dream?" Splinter News, September 10, 2014, https://splinternews.com/is-rape-the-price-to-pay-for-migrant-women-chasing-the-1793842446.

6 "Human Trafficking: Modern Enslavement of Immigrant Women in the United States," American Civil Liberties Union, accessed August 9, 2018, https://www.aclu.org/other/human-trafficking-modern-enslavement-immigrant-women-united-states.

7 Walter Ewing, Daniel E. Martínez, and Rubén G. Rumbaut, "The Criminalization of Immigration in the United States," American Immigration Council, July 13, 2015, www.americanimmigrationcouncil.org/research/criminalization-immigration-united-states.

8 Martin Luther King Jr., *Strength to Love* (Minneapolis: Fortress Press, 2010), 28–29.

9 Ibid., 29.

10 "The Three- and Ten-Year Bars," American Immigration Council, October 28, 2016, https://www.americanimmigrationcouncil.org/research/three-and-ten-year-bars.

Chapter 4

1 "Timeline: Guatemala's Brutal Civil War," PBS *Newshour*, March 7, 2011, https://www.pbs.org/newshour/health/latin_america-jan-june11-timeline_03-07.

2 Óscar Romero, *The Scandal of Redemption: When God Liberates the Poor, Saves Sinners, and Heals Nations* (Walden, NY: Plough Publishing House, 2018), 55.

Chapter 5

1 Ada María Isasi-Díaz, *Mujerista Theology: A Theology for the Twenty-First Century* (Maryknoll, NY: Orbis Books, 1996), 60.
2 Megan McKenna, *Not Counting Women and Children: Neglected Stories from the Bible* (Maryknoll, NY: Orbis Books, 1994), 178.
3 Isasi-Díaz, *Mujerista Theology*, 66.

Chapter 6

1 Robert Chao Romero, "Faith in the Life of César Chávez: Part I, 'Abuelita Theology,'" Radical Discipleship, October 30, 2016, https://radicaldiscipleship.net/2016/10/30/faith-in-the-life-of-cesar-chavez-part-i-abuelita-theology/.
2 Ada María Isasi-Díaz, *Mujerista Theology: A Theology for the Twenty-First Century* (Maryknoll, NY: Orbis Books, 1996), 137.
3 Ruth Haley Barton, *Sacred Rhythms* (Downers Grove, IL: InterVarsity Press, 2006), 22–24.

Chapter 7

1 Ann Klein and Mitch Smith, "Killing of Mollie Tibbetts in Iowa Inflames Immigration Debate," *New York Times*, August 22, 2018, https://www.nytimes.com/2018/08/22/us/mollie-tibbetts-cristhian-rivera.html.
2 G. J. Wenham, ed., *Genesis*, New Bible Commentary (Downers Grove, IL: InterVarsity Press, 2010), 86.
3 Frances Bernat, "Immigration and Crime," *Oxford Research Encyclopedia of Criminology*

and Criminal Justice, April 2017, DOI: 10.1093/acrefore/9780190264079.013.93.

4 "Victims of Criminal Activity: U Nonimmigrant Status," U.S. Citizenship and Immigration Services, last modified June 12, 2018, https://www.uscis.gov/humanitarian/victims-human-trafficking-other-crimes/victims-criminal-activity-u-nonimmigrant-status/victims-criminal-activity-u-nonimmigrant-status.

5 Wenham, *Genesis*, 86.

6 Richard Beck Jr., *Stranger God: Meeting Jesus in Disguise* (Minneapolis: Fortress Press, 2017), 27. Emphasis in the original.

7 Ibid., 12.

Chapter 8

1 Zuzana Cepla, "Fact Sheet: Family-Based Immigration," National Immigration Forum, February 14, 2018, https://immigrationforum.org/article/fact-sheet-family-based-immigration/.

Chapter 9

1 Lamar Williamson Jr., *Mark: Interpretation, A Biblical Commentary for Teaching and Preaching* (Louisville, KY: John Knox Press, 1983), 137.

2 Ched Myers, *Binding the Strong Man: A Political Reading of Mark's Story of Jesus* (Maryknoll, NY: Orbis Books, 2000), 203.

3 Ibid., 203–204.

4 Monika Fander, "Gospel of Mark: Women as True Disciples of Jesus," in *Feminist Biblical Interpretation:*

A Compendium of Critical Commentary of the Bible and Related Literature, ed. Luise Schottroff and Marie-Theres Wacker (Grand Rapids, MI: Eerdmans, 2012), 633.

5 Mitzi J. Smith, "Race, Gender, and the Politics of 'Sass': Reading Mark 7:24-30 through a Womanist Lens of Intersectionality and Inter(con)textuality," in *Womanist Interpretations of the Bible: Expanding the Discourse*, ed. Gay L. Byron and Vanessa Lovelace (Atlanta: SBL Press, 2016), 103.

6 David J. Cantor and Malte Plewa, "Forced Displacement and Violent Crime: A Humanitarian Crisis in Central America?," *Humanitarian Exchange* 69 (June 2017): 13.

7 José Miguel Cruz, "Trump Is Wrong about MS-13. His Rhetoric Will Make It Worse," *Washington Post*, January 31, 2018, https://www.washingtonpost.com/news/posteverything/wp/2018/01/31/trump-is-wrong-about-ms-13-and-his-rhetoric-will-make-it-worse/.

8 Ibid.

9 Williamson, *Mark*, 138.

10 Smith, "Race, Gender, and the Politics of 'Sass,'" in *Womanist Interpretations of the Bible*, 108.

11 Ibid., 104.

12 Ibid., 106.

13 Ched Meyers, "'Nothing from Outside Can Defile You!' Jesus' Embrace of the 'Other' in Mark 4–8," in *Our God Is Undocumented: Biblical Faith and Immigrant Justice*, by Ched Myers and Matthew Colwell (Maryknoll, NY: Orbis Books, 2012), 135, 137. Emphasis in the original.

14 Jim Puzzanghera, "There Now Are More Job Openings in the U.S. Than Workers to Fill Them," *Los Angeles*

Times, June 5, 2018, https://www.latimes.com/business/la-fi-job-openings-workers-20180605-story.html.

15 Julia Preston, "Immigrants Aren't Taking Americans' Jobs, New Study Finds," *New York Times*, September 21, 2016, https://www.nytimes.com/2016/09/22/us/immigrants-arent-taking-americans-jobs-new-study-finds.html.

16 Ibid.

17 Joel Rose, "Resettled Refugees Help to 'Bring Buffalo Back,'" NPR *Morning Edition*, December 2, 2015, https://www.npr.org/2015/12/02/458007064/resettled-refugees-help-to-bring-buffalo-back.

18 Smith, "Race, Gender, and the Politics of 'Sass,'" in *Womanist Interpretations of the Bible*, 108.

19 Ta-Nehisi Coates, *Between the World and Me* (New York: Spiegel and Grau, 2015), 97.

20 Smith, "Race, Gender, and the Politics of 'Sass,'" in *Womanist Interpretations of the Bible*, 108.

Chapter 10

1 Nicole Fernandez and Albert Inserra, "Disproportionate Number of ESL Students in Special Education Classes," *TESL-EJ: Teaching English as a Second or Foreign Language* 17, no. 2 (August 2013): http://www.tesl-ej.org/wordpress/issues/volume17/ej66/ej66a1/.

2 "The Dream Act, DACA, and Other Policies Designed to Protect Dreamers," American Immigration Council, September 6, 2017, https://www.americanimmigrationcouncil.org/research/dream-act-daca-and-other-policies-designed-protect-dreamers/.

3 Timothy Tennent, "Christian Perspective on Immigration," June 22, 2011, video, 5:19, https://www.youtube.com/watch?v=WHx95cuXpUE.

Chapter 11

1 Graham Stanton, *The Gospels and Jesus*, 2nd ed. (Oxford, UK: Oxford University Press, 2002), 66–67.

2 Stephen C. Barton, "The Gospel According to Matthew," *The Cambridge Companion to the Gospels*, ed. Stephen C. Barton (Cambridge, UK: Cambridge University Press, 2007), 124–25.

3 Ibid., 125.

4 Roger Daniels, *Guarding the Golden Door: American Immigration Policy and Immigrants since 1882* (New York: Hill and Wang, 2004), 204.

5 Reece Jones, *Violent Borders: Refugees and the Right to Move* (London: Verso, 2016), 6.

6 Ibid., 6–7.

7 Ibid., 5.

8 Ibid., 31.

9 Donald M. Kerwin Jr., "Migration, Development, and the Right Not to Have to Migrate in the New Era of Globalization," in *On "Strangers No Longer": Perspectives on the Historic U.S.-Mexican Catholic Bishops' Pastoral Letter on Migration*, ed. Todd Scribner and J. Kevin Appleby (Mahwah, NJ: Paulist Press, 2013), 143.

10 Ched Myers, "Gospel Nativities vs. Anti-Immigrant Nativism," in *Our God Is Undocumented: Biblical Faith and Immigrant Justice*, by Ched Myers and Matthew Colwell (Maryknoll, NY: Orbis Books, 2012), 171–72.

11 Ibid., 176.

The Author

Karen González is a speaker, writer, and immigrant advocate who works as the director of human resources for World Relief. An immigrant from Guatemala, González studied at Fuller Theological Seminary. She has worked in the nonprofit world for more than ten years and is a former public school teacher. González, who lives in Baltimore, has written about spiritual formation, Latinx identity, race, gender, the Enneagram, and immigration. Her work has been published in *Sojourners*, *Evangelicals for Social Action*, *Christ and Pop Culture*, *Christianity Today*, *Mutuality Magazine*, The Mudroom, and The Salt Collective. Connect with her at Karen-Gonzalez.com.

WITHDRAWN

CLARKSTON INDEPENDENCE
DISTRICT LIBRARY
6495 CLARKSTON ROAD
CLARKSTON, MI 48346-1501